D0506971

Morning Meeting

Messages

K-6

180

Sample Charts from
Three Classrooms

Rosalea S. Fisher, Eric Henry, Deborah Porter

Introduction by Marlynn K. Clayton

© 2006 by Northeast Foundation for Children, Inc.

All rights reserved. No part of this book may be reproduced in any form or by any electronic or mechanical means, including information storage and retrieval systems, without permission in writing from the publisher, except by a reviewer, who may quote brief passages in a review.

ISBN-13: 978-1-892989-17-8
ISBN-10: 1-892989-17-4

Library of Congress Control Number: 2006927094

Project manager: Jennifer Audley
Photographs: Peter Wrenn, Helen Merena, Cherry Wyman
Cover and book design: Helen Merena

Northeast Foundation for Children, Inc.
85 Avenue A, Suite 204
P. O. Box 718
Turners Falls, MA 01376-0718

800-360-6332
www.responsiveclassroom.org

10 09 08 07 06   6 5 4 3 2 1

ACKNOWLEDGMENTS

Many voices informed and many hands guided this book's development. By sharing their ideas, questions, and experiences with Northeast Foundation for Children over the past twenty-five years, thousands of teachers have helped shape our understanding of the full power of morning messages in enhancing elementary students' education. We are grateful for their contributions.

We'd also particularly like to thank:

Jen Audley, NEFC editor/writer, who served as project manager and editor.

Marlynn K. Clayton, NEFC co-founder and *Responsive Classroom* consulting teacher, who not only contributed the introduction, but also reviewed the entire manuscript.

Helen Merena, NEFC graphic designer, whose talents are evident on every page.

Alice Yang, NEFC publications manager, who shepherded the project through its early stages and then served as project mentor.

Roxann Kriete, NEFC executive director, for conceiving the idea for this book.

Mary Beth Forton, NEFC associate director, for organizing the initial collection of these charts and pitching in at several key junctures.

Julia Luteran and Gail Zimmerman, classroom practitioners and *Responsive Classroom* consulting teachers, who served as readers.

Many others at NEFC, including Lynn Bechtel, Ruth Sidney Charney, Paula Denton, Andy Dousis, Mike Fleck, Jay Lord, and Elizabeth Nash, who provided feedback and encouragement.

Lisa and Daniel Rodriguez-Ross, for checking the accuracy of the parts written in Spanish.

Janice Gadaire Fleuriel, for proofreading the manuscript.

Teachers, administrators, and children at Regional Multicultural Magnet School, New London, Connecticut; K.T. Murphy Elementary School, Stamford, Connecticut; Sheffield Elementary School, Turners Falls, Massachusetts; Six to Six Interdistrict Magnet School, Bridgeport, Connecticut; Reingold Elementary School, Fitchburg, Massachusetts; South Fitchburg Early Learning Center, Fitchburg, Massachusetts; Garrison Elementary School, Washington, D.C.; Washington Magnet School, West Haven, Connecticut; Hart Magnet School, Stamford, Connecticut; and Kensington Avenue Elementary School, Springfield, Massachusetts, who welcomed visitors into their schools to observe and photograph.

ADDITIONAL ACKNOWLEDGMENTS

I would like to acknowledge my husband, Dick, for his caring, encouragement, and patience for the long hours of work spent at school and at home. I would also like to acknowledge Michele Sabia, K.T. Murphy staff developer, for being my mentor and *my* teacher. Finally, I thank Ruth Sidney Charney and Chip Wood for the privilege of having their voices in my head and my heart. —ROSALEA S. FISHER

I would like to thank my students for making the classroom such a friendly, inviting, and exciting place to be each day. A great thank you to my teachers who have inspired me in countless ways: Raymond Carver, Joel Fink, Marlynn Clayton, Linda Crawford, Cathy Eli, and my fifth grade teacher, Mrs. Kornman from Seoul American Middle School. Finally, I am grateful to my friends and family for their love and support and most of all to my partner, Keith, for his love and devotion. —ERIC HENRY

I would like to thank all the children in my class who make the chart come alive each day with their drawings and ideas. I am continually inspired by their capacity to greet each new day with renewed energy and interest. —DEBORAH PORTER

TABLE OF CONTENTS

Introduction

M A R L Y N N   K .   C L A Y T O N

NEFC co-founder and Responsive Classroom® consulting teacher

> March 7, 2005
>
> Dear Invertebrate Investigators,
>
> Yesterday we continued our studies about invertebrates, and we put two types of food in our worm farm. Recall what you know about worms as we make new observations today.
>
> Make a prediction: How do you think the contents of the worm farm will have changed since yesterday?

THIS MESSAGE, WRITTEN IN LARGE LETTERS and placed prominently on a chart stand near the door, greets students in a fourth grade class as they walk into the room on a March morning. After taking off their coats and putting away their belongings, several students gather around the chart to read the message and see what's in store for the day ahead.

Some students softly read the words aloud, and others read silently. They chat about their predictions and take turns writing them in the space left at the bottom of the chart:

"The food will be gone."
"No change."
"They will eat some of both."

When these students are done at the chart, they move on to another morning activity and a new group of students moves in. It's a fluid process, rich with opportunities for social interactions, informal learning, and the building of classroom community and students' sense of competence.

After the morning arrival time, the teacher moves the chart into the meeting circle for the class's daily morning meeting. At the conclusion of the meeting, the morning message is the focal point of the conversation.

"Who would like to read today's message?" asks the teacher as she adjusts the chart stand beside her slightly so the message is visible to every child in the circle.

The children's attention shifts to the chart, and many hands go up. The teacher calls on Alonzo, who reads the message aloud.

After he finishes, the teacher says to the class, "You've put some predictions up here. What do you notice about them?" and takes a few responses. The class then hears several students describe how they came up with their predictions.

"So, we have a lot of different predictions," the teacher summarizes, "We'll get back to this topic after lunch, when you'll do some writing about your predictions before we look at the worms. We're going to start the day now with partner reading. Get your folder and your book and meet your partner at your reading spot." The class disperses, energized and ready for a day of learning.

A daily message, written by the teacher for the class and highlighting one aspect of the learning day ahead, is a highly effective technique for welcoming students into the classroom and generating their excitement and sense of competence as they begin the day. It can help set the tone for the day and be used to reinforce a wide range of academic skills. Implemented in a wide range of K–6 classroom settings, a morning message is a simple but powerful technique with an array of benefits for students.

This book features 180 examples of morning meeting messages selected over the course of a year from three public elementary school classrooms: a K–1 class in a small rural school, a third grade bilingual class in an urban setting, and a fifth grade class in the suburbs of a large city. It also features guidelines and tips for creating your own messages and using them as a tool for teaching your class.

Purposes of Morning Meeting Messages

There are multiple purposes for a daily message chart. The teachers featured in this book hold the following goals in mind when crafting their daily messages to students:

1. To welcome students to school
2. To set a positive tone for the day
3. To reinforce literacy and other academic skills
4. To encourage a sense of community
5. To send students into the day ready to learn

1. Welcome students to school

Seeing an attractive and interesting message waiting for them at the beginning of the day lets children know that their teacher is ready for them, has thought about the day ahead, and welcomes them to it. The message helps children make the daily shift from being their "home selves" to being members of their classroom community. Below is a sample chart from the K–1 classroom featured in this book that illustrates how a teacher uses the chart to welcome students to school.

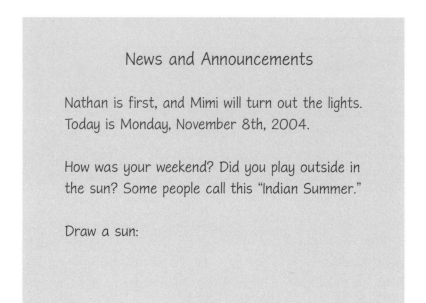

News and Announcements

Nathan is first, and Mimi will turn out the lights.
Today is Monday, November 8th, 2004.

How was your weekend? Did you play outside in
the sun? Some people call this "Indian Summer."

Draw a sun:

By asking students about their weekends and inviting each child to draw a sun, the teacher helps them make the transition from home to school and sends the message that each of their lives is important and each can make a valued contribution to classroom life.

2. Set a positive tone for the day

Another goal of the message is to excite the children about their academic day. The tone of the writing reflects the sense of community in the class—the feeling of "us." It conveys that the classroom is a fun, safe place for learning and working hard. It gives students an opportunity to feel competent and to see that their teacher believes in them and their abilities.

3. Reinforce literacy and other academic skills

Morning meeting messages give children the opportunity to practice functional reading every day. For children who are learning to read, messages that use predictable patterns and easy sight words provide high-interest, confidence-building practice. For more fluent readers, the message provides daily practice in reading harder words and sentences and reinforces the fact that reading is a valuable way to get information. The content is usually drawn from the math, science, literature, or other academic content the class is studying. Whatever the content, the text can also be used to reinforce literacy skills. Here, the third grade teacher in this book uses the message to give students practice in grasping units of measure.

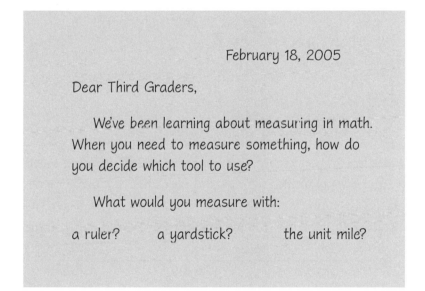

February 18, 2005

Dear Third Graders,

We've been learning about measuring in math. When you need to measure something, how do you decide which tool to use?

What would you measure with:

a ruler?   a yardstick?   the unit mile?

Besides using such a chart to discuss measuring, a teacher might also use it to lead the class in a quick, playful review of the spelling of "measure" versus "measuring" or the use of contractions.

4. Encourage a sense of community

A carefully crafted message is a tool for building a sense of community. It provides a context for acknowledging group accomplishments and challenges and can be used to prompt group thinking, planning, and reflection. A message can also serve as a mirror for the class when the teacher uses it to tell them positive things she or he has noticed about their learning and growth. In the message below, for example, the fifth grade teacher in this book reinforces the positive behaviors students showed in a class game:

11/18/04

Dear Cooperative Class,

Good morning! I was impressed by your focus and spirited play during yesterday's Explorer Matrix game. Wow! What are some things that you think made this activity go so well for us?

5. Send students into the day ready to learn

Reading and discussing the message together at the end of morning meeting helps students make the transition into the rest of the day. Because the content of the chart stems from the life and interests of the class, the message generates enthusiasm about the class's learning and launches students into the day with learning in mind.

The teachers who wrote the messages in this book are long-time teachers who use the *Responsive Classroom* approach to teaching and a daily morning meeting that uses the message as a teaching tool. (See the Appendix for information about the *Responsive Classroom* approach and its version of morning meeting.) While a daily morning message is part of the *Responsive Classroom* approach, all teachers, regardless of whether they use this approach to teaching, can use a morning message effectively.

The morning message charts selected from each of the three classrooms are intended to inspire you to create messages that meet the needs of your students and fit your teaching style. The messages featured in this book will give you ideas and guidance, but it is ultimately your knowledge of your class that will make the daily messages you write powerful, purposeful, and dynamic for your group of students.

How to Use This Book

- In addition to the 180 sample charts in this book, the next section provides general tips about creating and using messages. You may want to read these guidelines now, or wait until you have become familiar with the sample charts. Choose whichever order feels right for you.

- Although you will probably begin by perusing the charts from the grade level closest to the one you teach, remember to look at other grade levels for ideas that you can adapt to fit your class's needs and reading abilities.

- Look for common features among the sample messages, including length and other format issues, content that focuses on a single topic, and a tone that is friendly and inviting.

- Notice the differences in Deborah's, Rosalea's, and Eric's styles. Each of these teachers' messages are effective because they are authentic, reflecting her or his personality and relationship with a particular group of children.

- Pay attention to the way the messages change and evolve over the course of the school year. Look for threads and themes that emerge, and for evidence of the class's increasing skill and knowledge.

- Read the annotations to learn more about the thinking that guides the process of writing messages, as well as how teachers use messages during morning meeting and beyond.

Note: While the teachers' writing is the focus of the sample charts in this book, in some cases student responses have also been included. Where necessary, writing by students was edited to improve readability.

Tips for Creating and Using Morning Messages

WHILE EVERY TEACHER'S MESSAGE CHARTS will be unique and will reflect the personality of the class and the style of the teacher, there are some general guidelines that will help you create effective charts and make the best use of them in your teaching.

Recommendations for Materials

While a range of materials can be used to create morning messages, many teachers find that the most practical and effective materials are an easel stand, easel pad, and some colored markers. Some teachers opt to use the blackboard, whiteboard, an overhead projector, or even a computer screen projected on a wall. However, there are important advantages to the traditional easel pad and chart stand:

Easy to move around the room ■ At the beginning of the day, the message is usually placed where the children can easily see and work with it as they enter the room. Later, during morning meeting, the chart is placed in the seating circle. After the meeting, the chart may be moved to a less prominent spot in the room where children can continue to read or write on it. Most easel stands are easy to move in this way and are sturdy enough to hold up to the inevitable bumps that come with frequent moving.

Invites children to gather around and interact ■ An easel chart is inviting for children to look at and gather around. Some easels can be adjusted to be at children's eye level. And, easel paper is big enough for several children to write or draw on at the same time, which saves time and helps build a sense of community.

The writing is easy to read and doesn't smudge ■ Dark marker on white paper (newsprint quality paper is fine for this purpose) is generally easier on the eyes than projected images and facilitates reading, especially for beginning or struggling readers. Writing done with a marker also doesn't smudge the way chalk or dry-erase markers can. Writing with a marker therefore can help convey that the morning message is an important piece of work. Look for nontoxic and nonbleeding markers. Dark earth tones (blue, green, purple, brown) are easiest to read.

Allows the class to keep the charts ■ Unlike messages written on a dry-erase board or chalkboard, paper charts can last more than a day. This allows the class to use the charts to their full potential: Students can look back at charts from days, weeks, or months ago to remind themselves of past learning and reflect on their progress, and teachers can use past charts as springboards for extension activities.

Tips for Writing the Message

Write a message every day ■ There's power in writing a message to students every day. The predictability gives students a sense of security. In addition, when students see their teacher taking the time to write a message specifically to them every day, they get the idea that morning messages are important and deserving of their attention.

Write the message before students arrive ■ It's most effective to have the message chart ready for students to explore when they arrive in the room. The completed piece of writing communicates that their teacher is ready to start the day. This kind of morning message does not serve the same purpose as "language experience" approaches to teaching writing, where the teachers and students write together on chart paper. Nor is it meant as a place for students to practice responsibility by helping to create the message. With morning messages, the teacher is the author. The teacher decides what information to highlight and which skills to practice, and then writes the chart. The students' responsibility is to read the message and interact with it.

Focus on a single topic ■ Morning messages tend to focus on one topic, highlighting one important thing the class will do that day. Focusing on a single topic helps ensure that there will be enough time and focused energy for the teacher and class to have a meaningful but brief conversation about it during morning meeting. The goal is not to exhaust the topic during morning meeting, but to reveal an aspect of it.

Topics related to the class's academic work can derive from current literature, science, social studies, and math units. Classroom community issues, such as welcoming a new student or evaluating clean-up procedures, can make good topics from time to time. Message topics can also be drawn from class interests, such as writing plays, playing musical instruments, making inventions, preparing for school-wide events, or considering news from the outside world.

When choosing topics for message charts, consider:

Is it current? ▪ Each message is written for a specific group of children and addresses their classroom life at a specific place and time. Focusing on current work or building on work from previous days sets the stage for the day ahead.

Is it inclusive? ▪ Every message should speak to all the children in the group. Each student should see him/herself mirrored in the message.

Is it engaging? ▪ The most effective topics are those that are interesting to all students. Varying topics from day to day and using examples drawn from classroom life can help keep student interest high.

Think about literacy practice ■ Whatever the content you decide to include, consider how you can write the message to give children practice in the literacy skills they're learning. For example, can you embed vocabulary words in your sentences? Can you purposely use prefixes, suffixes, grammar and punctuation rules, or sentence structures they're learning? This literacy practice is most powerful when the skills are embedded in the text itself rather than added on as worksheet-style practice at the bottom of the chart.

Use a friendly tone ■ Using positive language offers children an image of themselves as strong, capable learners and valued members of a community. Positive attributes the class has demonstrated can be reinforced with greetings such as "Dear Cooperative Class" or "Good Morning, Successful Spellers!" as well as with specific, positive comments about work or behavior.

Even when there is a problem to discuss, the tone can be encouraging and empowering—for example, "I noticed some things were left on the floor in the cubby area the past few days. Let's plan together for how we can do a better job taking care of that area."

Aim for engagement ■ An inviting tone and meaningful activities can make any topic more engaging. For example, a message saying "We will be working on multiplication again today" might not inspire great engagement on its own. But if playful multiplication problems that involve events specific to classroom life are included, the message becomes much more exciting:

> Dear Merry Multipliers,
>
> Today we'll continue to work on our multiplication skills. I've noticed that you've really sharpened your thinking about it! Here's some fun multiplication that's happening right in our classroom:
>
> Yesterday during choice reading time, 7 of you read 5 pages, 6 of you read 7 pages, and 8 of you read 6 pages. How can we use multiplication to figure out how many pages we read?

Although each day's message should speak to the entire class, including students' names can be a way to draw them in to read the chart. Some teachers assign a role such as line leader each day and include the name of the person playing that role in the message. However names are included, it's important to use a fair system that ensures that all students will see their name written in the message over time.

Elements of Morning Messages

While each message chart is unique, all of the charts featured in this book contain the following elements:

Greeting ■ A salutation or heading opens the message. Many teachers use a letter salutation such as "Dear Second Graders," or "Good Morning, Friends!" No matter what the choice of words, the greeting is friendly in tone and tells the children, "This message is written especially for you! Come and read it!"

Date ■ The date may be recorded on the message in a variety of ways. For young children, using a consistent, predictable format is usually best. Many kindergarten and first grade teachers write the day and date in a simple sentence such as "Today is Tuesday, January 3, 2006." As children acquire calendar skills and learn the days of the week and the names of months, some teachers leave parts of the date blank and have the group fill them in during morning meeting.

In messages for more experienced readers, the date is usually located in a corner, as it would be in a letter. Students can benefit from seeing this information in a variety of formats: with and without abbreviations, or in "shorthand" such as 2/27/06.

Body of the message ■ The body of the message is written in a style that is developmentally appropriate for the children in the class. With the exception of very beginning readers, students should be able to read and understand at least parts of the message before morning meeting, either independently or with assistance.

Kindergarten and First Grade

Messages for beginning readers generally use easy sight words and very simple sentences, often with predictable, repeating patterns. Messages for children who cannot read at all yet may use just a few words and simple pictures to aid comprehension. As with messages for all grades, every day the message says something fun and engaging about that day's learning or about the classroom community. For example, the message one day might be:

> Maria is first.
> Moses is the caboose.
> Today is Monday.
> Do you like to paint?

The next day, the message might be:

> John is first.
> Sarah is the caboose.
> Today is Tuesday.
> We will sing a song.

The predictable patterns in the beginning sentences help students read them independently. The final sentence varies from the predictable pattern. This gives students a chance to practice decoding with text that is very meaningful to them. As the children's word recognition and decoding skills grow, new words appear, other sentence patterns are introduced, and eventually simple sentences are connected to make compound sentences.

Second and Third Grades

For children making the shift from "learning to read" to "reading to learn," messages begin having more fluid sentence structures, compound sentences, and distinct paragraphs. Many teachers at these levels write their message in the form of a letter to the class.

Fourth, Fifth, and Sixth Grades

In the upper elementary grades, the message models the kind of writing expected of students or echoes the types of writing they might find in their reading. Sentence structures vary from simple to complex, and letter format is generally used. The teacher's language shows respect and recognition of students' maturity; a simple switch from "Good Morning, Children" to "Good Morning, Students" or "Good Morning, Learners" can go a long way.

Optional Elements
The following elements, while seen in many of the charts in this book, are considered optional:

Related tasks ■ The body of the message may conclude with a question to think about or a simple activity for students to complete on the chart before the meeting starts. Such tasks are most effective when they go hand in hand with the body, inviting students to interact with what they've read in some way. For example, in the scene that opens the introduction to this book, the task "Make a prediction: What do you think we will see?" is related to the opening sentences of the morning message.

One key to creating related tasks that inspire feelings of capability in children is to resist using them to teach brand new material or skills. The message is a place for quick warm-ups and confident skill practice. The tasks that work best are those that everyone in the group will be able to complete quickly, independently, and successfully.

When children write on this part of the chart, the goal is not perfect spelling, capitalization, punctuation, or grammar, though students should try their best. The emphasis in this area of the chart should be on students' self-expression rather than on writing mechanics.

Closing and signature ■ Many teachers who write messages in letter format use a closing that's in a respectful and professional voice, such as "Sincerely," or "Your teacher," followed by their name or signature. Some teachers conclude with an encouraging phrase such as "Let's have a great learning day!" or "Do your best!" The choice depends on what feels authentic and makes sense for a particular class.

Announcements ■ While the date is always included in the message, information about the daily schedule usually is not. The emphasis is on topics that encourage thinking and learning, not on classroom logistics. Most teachers have a place in the classroom for notices such as "Today is Music" or for the list of who will be sharing during meeting that day. In cases where it's truly necessary for children to see such notes before morning meeting, you can write them succinctly in a corner of the chart designated as a "News Corner."

Class riddles ■ As a way to foster engagement and help class members know each other better, some teachers regularly include "class riddles"—challenge questions such as "Who has a new pet that has feathers?" or "How many people in our class have only brothers?" These encourage children to pay attention to and remember facts their classmates have shared. If you use class riddles—or name students in the charts in other ways—it's essential to name all students with equal frequency.

Some Mechanical Considerations

Color ■ Some teachers write the text of the message in one dark color, and then use additional colors to highlight and decorate the chart. Other teachers, especially in the primary grades, use a different color for each sentence or each paragraph. While the intent behind using different colors is to help children see distinct sentences or paragraphs, it can be visually over-stimulating and may lead to over-dependence on the color cues. Message text written in a single, solid color allows students to practice using the standard cues that delineate sentences and paragraphs: capitalization, punctuation, and indentation.

Teacher handwriting ■ Neat, legible handwriting in a style that all students in the class can read says to the students, "This chart is important class work, and it's for everyone." Once students have mastered cursive, using it in the chart provides them with an opportunity to practice reading script.

Accurate spelling, punctuation, and grammar ▪ Since students use the message to practice reading, it's important that all spelling, grammar, punctuation, and capitalization be correct. This applies to all writing that the teacher does in the message and to writing by students who fill in missing letters, numbers, or words in the body of the message on behalf of the group. An exception is when the teacher deliberately includes errors in the text and then invites students to find and correct those mistakes.

Guidelines for Using Morning Messages in the Classroom

The following guidelines assume the teacher uses the message as part of a daily morning meeting as used in the *Responsive Classroom®* approach to teaching. (For a summary of this particular type of morning meeting, see the Appendix. For in-depth information, see *The Morning Meeting Book* by Roxann Kriete.) However, teachers can use the morning message as a teaching tool during any part of the school day. It could be used in a literacy workshop, a reading group, or a whole class meeting of any type.

Before morning meeting ▪ For most classes, the general expectation is that students will have read the message by the time morning meeting begins. Often this is one of several tasks that students are expected to complete at the beginning of the day. If the number and complexity of these tasks is manageable, reading the morning message can usually fit comfortably into this time. If students generally all arrive at the same time, at the beginning of the year the group learns and practices strategies for turn-taking and keeping the area around the chart from becoming too crowded.

On days when some students arrive later than others, children will have varying amounts of time to work with the message. One approach is to enlist early arrivers and stronger readers to help classmates read the chart and craft their responses.

Another approach is to prioritize the morning tasks. This might mean telling students that if they arrive late, the message is the first thing they should do. Or it might mean that working with the message before morning meeting is a choice rather than a requirement. In that case, students may benefit from having time later in the day to add their responses to the chart.

Whatever the expectations are for working with the message in the morning, it's important to teach them explicitly at the beginning of the year. Model the procedure

students are to use and give them chances to practice before expecting them to carry out the routine independently.

During morning meeting ▪ Most classes begin the final segment of morning meeting by turning their attention as a group to the message for a few minutes. Varying the way the message is read from day to day can keep things interesting. Choral reading, line-by-line "echo" reading, teacher or individual student reading, and individual student summarizing or paraphrasing can all work well. So can reading at different volumes or with different intonations, such as using whispery, serious, or musical voices. When the message asks for written responses, some teachers have students read the responses they wrote; it can also be effective to have students read each other's responses aloud or simply share what they notice about the responses as a whole.

This reading is followed by a brief discussion or activity that expands on the content of the message. This is a critical part of the process. It's an opportunity for the class to explore thinking questions posed in the message, comment on the message content,

Ways to Make Writing Daily Messages Easier

AT FIRST, WRITING A MESSAGE EVERY DAY MAY SEEM DAUNTING. With practice, most teachers find that it becomes easier, usually taking only a few minutes per day. The following tips may help:

- *Use a weekly schedule.* For example, Monday's message can always be about events from the weekend, while Tuesday's focus can always be on science. Wednesdays can be language arts days, Thursdays can be humor days, and Fridays can always feature a math-related topic. Also, some teachers plan a week's messages as they do their lesson-planning for that week.

- *Make notes or a draft the day before.* Some teachers write the next day's message at the end of the day, while others prefer to write when they arrive in the morning. Either way, planning ahead cuts down on the stress of trying to think and write under time pressure. Try creating a rough draft on normal letter-sized paper, or simply jot down your ideas and leave a sticky note for yourself on the chart pad.

- *Keep it simple.* Messages don't have to be creative masterpieces. Teachers who pressure themselves to write a lot or to be clever, funny, or artistic often end up with a routine they cannot sustain. Remember that the goal is to engage students, not to entertain them. Speaking directly to the class about things they care about is usually the best way to get their interest.

- *Share ideas with colleagues.* A quick conversation can help you overcome "writer's block," and may generate topics for future messages as well. Reflecting with a colleague on how a message worked can be inspiring, too. Although you will each be writing messages tailored to your own classes, collaboration can be a great way to get ideas and keep things fun.

engage in the literacy skill practice embedded in the message, and perhaps add to any written responses they made on the chart. Directing the discussion in ways that maximize participation—for instance, using group answering strategies such as "thumbs up, thumbs down" or "Me, too!" gestures—gets the whole group involved.

After morning meeting ■ Many teachers leave the message chart on display for the rest of the school day. This allows students to continue adding ideas. The message might also be used during lessons later in the day.

Some primary grade teachers save morning messages and add them to their classroom libraries. Some send the day's message home with a different child each day, a practice that can build the home-school connection. Middle and upper elementary grade teachers use messages as classroom resources, too. A message that asks, "What do you know about salmon?" might be posted on a wall so that students can add answers for the duration of their salmon study. Over time, the document becomes a testament to the class's learning.

One especially powerful teaching idea is to save all of the charts for a year and use them to launch a year-end assessment project. Simply spreading out as many of the charts as you can in a large space such as a gym provides a powerful visual narrative of a year in community. By walking around and looking at all the charts, students can recall the year and see evidence of their learning and accomplishments.

———————————————————————

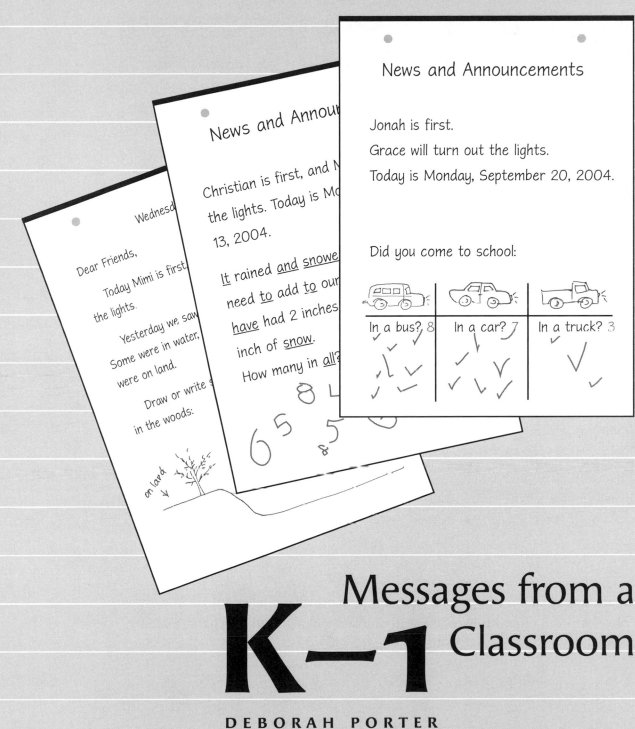

News and Announcements

Jonah is first.

Grace will turn out the lights.

Today is Monday, September 20, 2004.

Did you come to school:

In a bus? 8	In a car? 7	In a truck? 3

News and Annour...

Christian is first, and N...
the lights. Today is Mo...
13, 2004.

It rained and snowe...
need to add to our...
have had 2 inches...
inch of snow.

How many in all?

6 5 8

Wednesd...

Dear Friends,

Today Mimi is first...
the lights.

Yesterday we, saw...
Some were in water,...
were on land.

Draw or write...
in the woods:

on land

K–1 Messages from a Classroom

DEBORAH PORTER

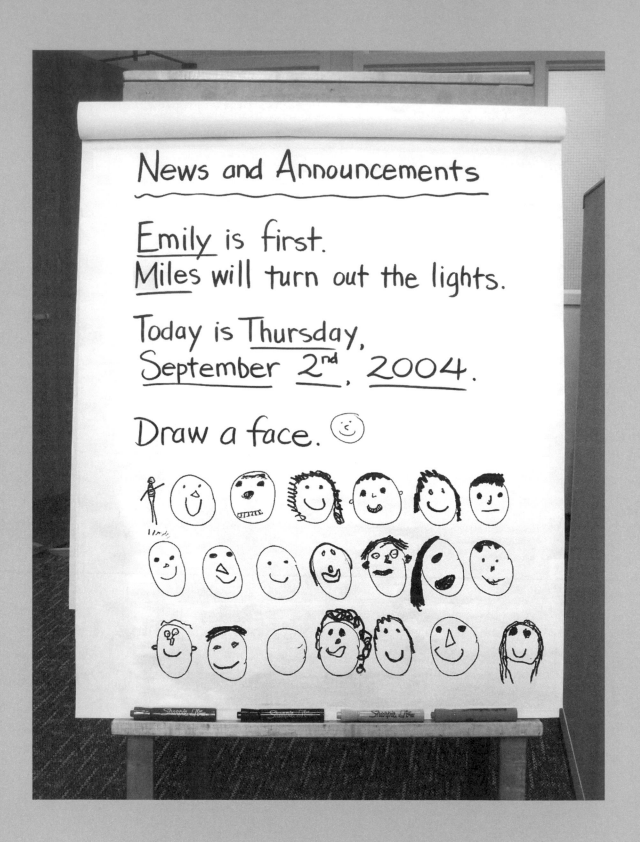

Morning Message Gets Us Ready for the Day

DEBORAH PORTER

K–1 teacher, Heath Elementary School, Heath, Massachusetts

WRITING THE MORNING MEETING MESSAGE is a daily routine that I rely upon to focus myself after the rush of getting ready for the day. As I do my daily planning, ideas for the message emerge from what we will be learning, as well as what's going on in the school, in town, or even in the environment. By the time I actually write the message I have a very good idea of what to say, and it takes only a few minutes. As I begin, all the hubbub of the morning falls away while I think about the children and our work together. Writing the message serves me in the same way that it serves the children: as my transition from home to school. When the children come into the room, I am ready to welcome them, knowing that everything is ready to go.

As they arrive, small groups of children take turns gathering at the chart. They want to know who has which job today and what the message says about the day ahead. They know we will be talking about it at morning meeting, and although they may not be able to read the entire message, many try to figure out as much as they can on their own. Others seek out the readers in the group for help.

The children also know there will usually be something for them to do at the bottom of the chart: a survey question, a skill to practice, or sometimes simply a decoration to add. It usually takes each child only a couple of minutes to draw or write on the chart, yet this helps them focus on the day and become excited about what it might bring. Within minutes there is a buzz in the air as children eagerly show their friends what they have drawn or the fancy letter they have made.

The message has many roles in our classroom. It serves as an anchor to our learning. We use it to document our work and to start conversations where both personal interests and curriculum are relevant. It helps create our common ground. The chart is also part of our history together. We often refer to it throughout the day and go back to previous days' charts to reflect on something we've discussed earlier.

We also use the chart to practice skills. Because the format is predictable, reading the message together allows the children to practice fluency and to try out the reading strategies they are learning. During our meeting time, there are opportunities for children at varying skill levels to contribute. One child might know a whole word, another the letter sound we need, and still another might remember something about what we are doing that day that helps us figure out what the message says.

School and Classroom Demographics

Heath Elementary is a small public school in a rural area of western Massachusetts. We have just over 100 students in pre-K through sixth grade. Heath Elementary opened ten years ago after a decade of community effort to reestablish a school in the small town of Heath. As a classroom teacher and a town resident, I find great pleasure in being part of a learning community that encompasses children, parents, staff, and townspeople.

About two-thirds of the school's students come from Heath, and the rest from elsewhere in the county as school-of-choice students. The student population is predominantly white, but there is marked socioeconomic diversity among the families. Many of the students qualify for free or reduced-price lunch, while some are from quite affluent families. The geographic isolation of our community means that families who live in poverty here often rely heavily on the school for services.

During the year from which the following morning meeting charts were taken, the class included eighteen children. There were six girls and twelve boys—half were kindergartners and half were first graders. The first graders had been with me the year before, so they began school knowing the structure of the day and experienced in the routines and problem-solving approaches of this classroom. They took on a special role as buddies to the new kindergartners and

were great teachers when it came to passing on those routines and experiences. We also had a kindergarten classroom aide, Michelle Howe, who was with us most days.

The Children's Academic and Social Abilities

Among this group of children, there was the range of ability one would expect in any class, with some children unable to write their names yet and others already reading. However, this class in general was hard working, enjoyed books, and was eager to learn. Although there were the usual upsets over having to share and take turns, the children generally showed courage when facing the challenges of learning difficult things, forgiving those who forgot the rules, and working on being friendly toward everyone. They had a great sense of adventure in tackling classroom work and the readiness to share opinions and show compassion that is so characteristic of their age.

Our class included a few children with special needs who required individual accommodations. The class worked hard to understand their challenges and include them in our daily work as much as possible. Sometimes we relied on experts coming into the room, which meant adjusting to the way this changed the flow of the day. Always, we were learning ways to communicate with these classmates in ways that were respectful, friendly, and inclusive.

We all had to contend with a busy schedule that sometimes made our work time too short and our day choppy. One particular challenge relating to the message resulted from our schedule. Every morning right after morning meeting, the first graders were pulled out for language arts instruction with the reading/Title I teacher, Cathy

Geyster. Therefore, the message often referred to things happening after lunch, when the whole class would be together again.

Many times the questions asked during morning meeting and the thinking they'd inspired would have been forgotten by then. On the positive side, this schedule led us to refer to the chart throughout the day more than my classes from previous years had. We reread, revisited, and played with the words of the chart far more thoroughly and frequently, and we used the chart to refocus when we got distracted or off track.

My Teaching Approach

I've been teaching for over thirty years—all at the primary and preschool levels. I believe that learning must actively engage children, drawing them in to explore, experiment, and know the world around them. I plan and organize each day with this in mind. I feel that by focusing on the process of learning, rather than finished work, I am able to more clearly understand the learning needs of each child and, more importantly, to help each child know him/herself as a learner.

My approach to teaching comes from my knowledge of child development and a firm belief in every child's ability to make positive contributions to a community. The classroom and curriculum offer many ways for children to contribute. I hold both high academic and high social standards for the children I teach; at the same time, I'm committed to creating a learning community where it is possible to take risks, make mistakes, and explore honest differences.

A primary goal of my teaching is to foster independence and active learning. Because of this, it's important that everyone contributes to the well-being of our class. Every day, the children are challenged to learn and practice respectful ways to treat each other and their environment. Sharing ideas and materials, empathizing and cooperating, listening, solving problems, and taking responsibility for their own work are major areas of focus.

Morning meeting and the message chart are part of the foundation upon which this community is built. With the chart, we set the tone for learning, make the transition from home to school, talk about and plan our work, and review academic skills. Once we've worked with the chart together, we know we're ready for the day.

News and Announcements
Emily is first.
Margaret will turn out the lights.
Today is Wednesday, October 13, 2004.
Last night one of our spiders died. Why do you think that happened?
Make a spider to remember her by.
Sharpie

On the first day of school in this class, the message is addressed primarily to the returning first graders who remember working with messages from the previous year. Deborah titles the message "News and Announcements" to connect it with the section of morning meeting when the group will focus on it.

News and Announcements

August 31, 2004

Dear Friends,

Welcome back to school!

Today Nathan will be first, and Gus will turn out the lights.

Your teachers,

Ms. Porter, Ms. Howe,

and Ms. Geyster

Make a flower in the garden.

Deborah drew a flower as an example and the children added flowers in many styles and sizes.

Like many teachers, Deborah assigns particular students to be "first" (in line, for example) and to turn out the lights each day. Excitement about who will do these coveted jobs attracts children to the message and helps them learn to read each others' names.

News and Announcements

<u>Emily</u> is first.

<u>Miles</u> will turn out the lights.

Today is <u>Thursday</u>, <u>September</u> 2nd, <u>2004</u>.

Draw a face:

By the third day of school, all students have been taught to look for the chart in the morning, and the class has begun reading the message together in morning meeting, so now the message uses simple words and a predictable pattern.

Deborah shows the children that some of the words in the message are the same each day. They look for words in the message that will change (daily, monthly, and annually) and underline them together.

At the beginning of the year, Deborah teaches students how to complete tasks on the chart before expecting them to do it independently. Skills taught might include how to use markers, turn-taking, and knowing how many people can work at the chart stand at one time.

The class continues to pay attention to words that will change in the predictable text of the message. Today Deborah and the children draw boxes around them.

Deborah uses "Do you like … ?" questions about food preferences on many consecutive days at the beginning of the year. The repeating format and illustrations help beginning readers figure out what the message says. Deborah also uses the information to decide what the class will have for snack.

News and Announcements

April is first.

Christian will turn out the lights.

Today is Tuesday, September 7th, 2004.

Do you like peanut butter?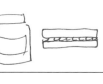

Yes	No
✓ ✓ ✓ ✓ ✓ ✓ ✓	✓ ✓ ✓ ✓ ✓

Using checkmarks to respond saves time. Once Deborah has taught the class how to make and use checkmarks, she can tell them to use this style of answering by simply putting a sample checkmark on the chart.

News and Announcements

Jonah is first.

Grace will turn out the lights.

Today is Monday, September 20, 2004.

Did you come to school:

In a bus? 8   In a car? 7   In a truck? 3

At the beginning of the year, morning messages that help the children learn about each other can be especially engaging and help build community.

Once the children have practiced answering "yes or no" questions for a while, other formats are introduced gradually. Here, the children choose among three responses instead of two, but the question itself is straightforward. They might use the totals later in a math lesson.

During morning meeting the class reads the message together and decides what number to write in the blank space. Then Deborah writes it.

There are many ways to have the group read the message. At the beginning of the year, Deborah and the students together figure out the unfamiliar words. Then the person who is first uses a pointer to guide the class as they read in unison. Later in the year, the child may choose to read the message on his or her own, with a classmate, a teacher, or everyone.

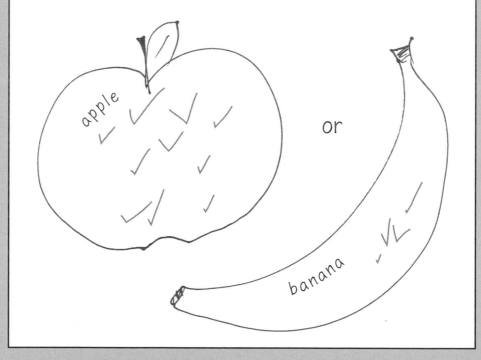

News and Announcements

Henry is first.

Autumn will turn out the lights.

Today is Tuesday, September 21st, 2004.

Which do you like better?

apple

or

banana

News and Announcements

Isabel is first.

Jonah will turn out the lights.

Today is Monday, September <u>27</u>th, 2004.

What is the first letter of your name?

Put it in a star.

Before long many children can "read" the repeating sentences at the beginning and can figure out what to do at the bottom of the chart before the meeting.

In this task, Deborah expects that the children will know which letter to write; the challenge is to fit their writing into a defined space.

News and Announcements

Christian is first.

David will turn out the lights.

Today is Tuesday, September <u>28</u>, 2004.

Did you see our caterpillars?

T t

Messages can be very simple and do not have to include written responses by students. Here, the box around the question draws children's attention to it, and the topic is sure to engage their curiosity. Some may be able to read the boxed question on their own, but everyone reads it during the meeting, when they'll also share what they noticed about the caterpillars.

Teachers sometimes have students practice finding letters in the message, as Deborah has here with the letters "t" and "T." She highlights each letter they find.

News and Announcements

Cody is first.

Isabel will turn out the lights. Today is Thursday, September 30, 2004.

Are you

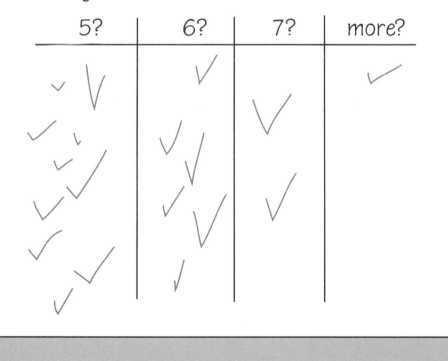

5?	6?	7?	more?

To increase the reading challenge, Deborah varies the format of the predictable part of the message slightly by beginning the third sentence on the second line. During meeting, discussion of this change reinforces that the words are still the same; only their position has changed.

News and Announcements

Timmy is first.

Robin will turn out the lights. Today

is Tuesday, October <u>12</u>, 2004.

Did you see the leaves?

What is happening?

Make a leaf.

Deborah often includes questions in the body of the message. Children are not expected to write answers to those questions; often, the group discusses their ideas about them during morning meeting.

Questions that encourage children to observe their surroundings with curiosity and interest work well because all children can answer them successfully.

Deborah teaches the children to respond in writing only at the bottom of the chart and designs that part of the message so children can answer regardless of their writing ability. In this case, the children drew leaves and colored them green, yellow, orange, red, and brown.

News and Announcements

Emily is first.

Margaret will turn out the lights.

Today is Wednesday, October <u>13</u>, 2004.

Last night one of our spiders died. Why
do you think that happened?

Make a spider to remember her by.

Once the class has become accustomed to seeing the new way of formatting these sentences, occasionally going back to the old way can help them develop flexibility and improve reading skills.

The children drew spiders of many different colors, shapes, and sizes. Deborah's example reinforces what the class had learned about spider anatomy by showing eight legs and a distinct head and body. The children's drawings include similar details. (See a photograph of this chart on page 27.)

This task could take a long time if every student were expected to respond before morning meeting. Remember that you can make responding on the chart a choice, then allow students to continue adding to the chart later in the day.

The message prompts children to prepare for the day's activity by making predictions. Students drew trees with branches and leaves, salamanders, a bird on a tree trunk, and other animals. Discussion during meeting might involve adding to this list or thinking about other aspects of what a day outdoors will be like.

News and Announcements

Grace is first.

April will turn out the lights. Today is Monday, October <u>18</u>, 2004.

ALL SCHOOL HIKE!

What do you think we will see? Draw your idea.

News and Announcements

Margaret is first.

Nathan will turn out the lights. Today is Thursday, October 21, 2004.

Today your parents will come for a conference. What do you think I should tell them about our work together?

Practice the ABCs:

A B C D E F G H I J K L M N
O P Q R S T U V W X Y Z

The children would share their ideas about this question during morning meeting. By inviting the children's input, Deborah reinforces their sense of community and raises their awareness about the importance of the work they do in school.

Once they have been introduced to the idea of "practice" and why it's important, tasks focused on practice can be good warm-ups for children at this level. An activity such as this would have been done during language arts for several days beforehand, so the children would know what to do when they saw it.

News and Announcements

Robin is first.

Grant will turn out the lights. Today is

Friday, October 22nd, 2004.

Today let's remember to take the

caterpillar chrysalis outside. How do

you think it will stay warm in winter?

Vocabulary challenges in the message work best when the word has already been introduced and children are familiar with it. Here, the class has been studying caterpillars and has learned the word "chrysalis," so Deborah is confident that some children will recognize it on their own. She also knows they all will delight in figuring out this grown-up word when they read the chart together.

News and Announcements

Ba(s)il is fir(s)t.

Timmy will turn (o)ut the light(s.) Today i(s)

Tuesday, (O)ctober <u>26</u>, 2004.

H(o)w many seed(s)d(o) y(o)u think these

pumpkin(s) have?   440   308

100 (○) (○)   1 (○)0 (○)(○)(○) 0

91   1018   1000 (○)
                           (○)
                            99

1(○)(○)(○)(○)(○)(○)

It's not necessary for every child to respond in writing each day. In this case, a few answers give the class plenty to talk about at meeting, and others can add their guesses later.

Using the message for letter or word searches can be a quick, confidence-building activity at many times of day. Students will need to practice this before they can do it independently.

When Deborah first begins to combine the first and second sentences in the message, she formats it so that there is only one change: the ", and" replaces the period at the end of the first sentence. The position of the other words doesn't change.

A meaningful task that involves voting helps the children understand what "voting day" means and helps them think about the more abstract question asked in the body of the message. During morning meeting they will talk about voting day and what they know about this event.

News and Announcements

April is first, and

David will turn out the lights. Today is

Tuesday, November <u>2</u>, 2004.

Today is voting day in America! Why

do you think people will vote?

Vote for tomorrow's snack.

To reinforce learning about vowels, the vowels in the message are written in a different color.

News and Announcements

Nathan is first, and Mimi will turn out the lights. Today is Monday, November 8th, 2004.

How was your weekend? Did you play outside in the sun? Some people call this "Indian Summer."

Draw a sun:

A few days later, the new compound sentence flows across the page without artificial line breaks.

The children drew suns of many shapes and sizes. At meeting, Deborah might ask if anyone knows why this is called "Indian Summer."

Deborah reinforces learning about punctuation for the ends of sentences by emphasizing periods and question marks and pointing them out when they read the message.

News and Announcements

Mimi is first, and Alexander will turn out the lights. Today is Monday, November 22nd, 2004.

Nathan is 7 years old today. I wonder how we can figure out how old he will be in 3 years?

Help us plan. What kind of pie do you like best?

apple pie	cherry pie	blueberry pie	No, thank you!
			✓
✓ ✓ ✓	✓	✓ ✓	✓
✓ ✓ ✓	✓ ✓	✓	✓

The class might work on solving this math problem together quickly during the meeting. Or students could be asked to think about it until later in the day.

This task gives Deborah information that will help her plan for pie-making in the near future. It also helps the children understand what it means to plan—something Deborah will ask them to do more of as the year goes on.

News and Announcements

Margaret is first, and Cody will turn out the lights. Today is Tuesday, November 23rd, 2004.

We will make pie today.

How many 🍎 apples do you think go in an apple pie?

Make an estimate.

5 or 6	50	51	11	6 or 7
10	7	7	6 or 7	7
9	7	4	51	

Deborah might refer to the previous day's chart to show the class that since apple was the type of pie most people preferred, that is the type they will make today.

The class has been learning about making estimates, and Deborah emphasizes the word on the chart. Students might talk about how they decided on their estimates during meeting. Later when they actually make the pie, they would compare the estimates with the actual number of apples used.

News and Announcements

Amy is first, and Trish will turn out the lights. Today is Tuesday, November <u>30</u>, 2004.

We will be museum explorers. What do you think an explorer does?

Put yourself on the bus!

This message helps the class start thinking about what it will be like to go on a field trip, including the bus ride. At morning meeting, the class will talk about what they will do as "explorers."

News and Announcements

Miles is first, and Grant will turn out the lights. Today is Wednesday, December 1st, 2004.

Goodbye, November.
Hello, December!

What did you like at the Eric Carle Museum?

The task encourages children to reflect on the trip they took the day before. They had experience using Venn diagrams, so they knew that placing a checkmark in the intersecting area meant "I liked both."

A simple question can encourage active thinking. With this question Deborah gives the children something they can consider now and learn more about later when they go to the puppet show.

The task gives the children a chance to practice applying terms they have been learning to an event taking place outside their classroom.

News and Announcements

Jonah is first, and Gus will turn out the lights. Today is Monday, December <u>6</u>, 2004.

We will go to a puppet show.
The show is "Hansel and Gretel."
How do you think they will make the puppets move?

Is "Hansel and Gretel"

fiction?	or	nonfiction?

News and Announcements

Emily is first, and Justin will turn out the lights. Today is Tuesday, December 7, 2004.

Were you surprised when you looked out the window today?

How much snow do you think we got?

less than 2 inches	more than 2 inches

✓ ✓ ┌─┐
  │2│
  ├─┤
  │1│
  └─┘
✓ ✓ ✓ ✓ ✓ ✓ ✓
	✓ ✓ ┌─┐
	  │3│
	  ├─┤
	  │2│
	  ├─┤
	  │1│
	  └─┘ ✓ ✓ ✓

Each square on Deborah's original illustrations measured one square inch. By representing the units accurately, Deborah made it possible for children who did not yet have a concept of how big inches are to respond successfully.

Now that the class has been practicing measuring snow for a while, they solve a word problem using data they have collected. During meeting, children who wrote answers might be asked to explain how they arrived at them. Then the whole class would work together to agree upon a final answer.

News and Announcements

Christian is first, and Mimi will turn out the lights. Today is Monday, December 13, 2004.

It rained and snowed some more. We need to add to our weather chart. We have had 2 inches + 1 inch + 1 inch + 1 inch of snow.
How many in all?

6 5 8 4 4 7 2 6
8 5 6 4 4 8 5

Later in the day, Deborah and a small group of children find and underline sight words in the message.

News and Announcements

Jonah is first, and Gus will turn out the lights. Today is Tuesday, January 4, 2005.

Did you notice any new things in our room? New things for a new year!

Practice writing 2005:

2005   2005   2005

2005   2005

2005 2005

This message encourages children returning from vacation to reconnect with the classroom by looking for changes, and reinforces the concept of "the new year" in a variety of ways.

Children usually enjoy recognizing names in the message. Names can be important sight words for beginning readers; including them in the body of the message can be very motivating.

Justin is first, and Nathan will turn out the lights. Today is Tuesday, January 11th, 2005.

Grant's mom will do movement in the gym with the kindergarten while the first graders have art.

Many teachers include "secret word" or "secret message" activities on their charts. A student decides on a message and whispers it to the teacher, who writes it, leaving blanks to be filled in. The class works together during meeting to solve the puzzle.

secret message
Margaret said, "I like art!"

News and Announcements

Mimi is first, and April will turn out the lights. Today is Thursday, January 13th, 2005.

This afternoon we have music. We have a new teacher. Her name is Ms. Hanna.

Today you will draw a picture of how big you were when you were born. How big is that?

Using the message to give information about new teachers and other major changes in routine can help children feel secure. This message helps children get excited about meeting their new music teacher.

However, so the children's attention isn't entirely pulled away from the classroom, Deborah includes information about work that will happen inside the classroom as well.

News and Announcements

Basil is first, and Alexander will turn out the lights. Today is Thursday, January 20th, 2005.

Brrr! Another cold day!

Today we will work on our baby dolls. What do you think a baby needs to grow up healthy?

Happy Birthday, David!

Where were you born?

Massachusetts	Somewhere else
Alexander Gus	Ms. Porter
Nathan Cody	Emily
MILES Mimi	Basil
Justin Isabel GRACE	Timmy
April CHRISTIAN	MARGARET
Grant	
Jonah DAVID	

As the class works on this multi-day project, Deborah uses the message to help the children gather information about what they were like as babies and compare it to what they are like now.

Deborah writes her name to show the students that she wants them to answer the question with names rather than checkmarks. During morning meeting, the people who were not born in Massachusetts might say where they were born.

News and Announcements

Isabel is first, and Timmy will turn out the lights. Today is Tuesday, January 25th, 2005.

We got a letter from Robin! I wonder what it says? Let's read it together.

Is your baby doll done?

yes	no
Gus Cody Emily	Mimi DAVID
Jonah GRACE	Timmy
Isabel	Basil
Justin Grant	Nathan
April	AlexANder
CHRISTIAN MILES	
MARGARET	

Finding and circling vowels in the message is a quick review activity later in the day.

The letter (from a student who had moved away) was attached to the message chart so students could see it before the group read it together.

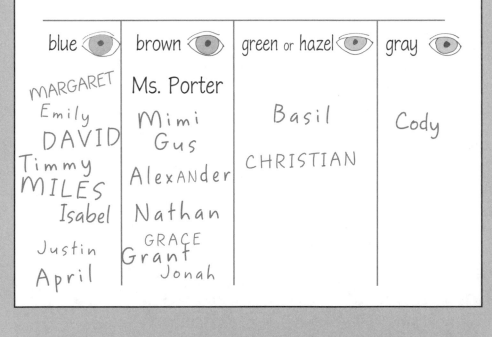

News and Announcements

April is first, and David will turn out the lights.
Today is Friday, January <u>28</u>th, 2005.

Yesterday we made a graph to show how big
you were when you were born. Let's make one
for eye color today.

What color are your eyes?

For each eye illustration, Deborah used the corresponding color for the iris. The information collected here is used in several ways: making a graph later in the day, coloring the eyes of the dolls, and learning about similarities and differences among members of the class.

blue 👁	brown 👁	green or hazel 👁	gray 👁
MARGARET	Ms. Porter		
Emily	Mimi	Basil	Cody
DAVID	Gus		
Timmy	AlexANder	CHRISTIAN	
MILES	Nathan		
Isabel	GRACE		
Justin	Grant		
April	Jonah		

News and Announcements

Cody is first, and Jonah will turn out the lights. Today is Tuesday, February 1, 2005.

Goodbye, January.
Hello, February.

Think:

What do you know about February?

Feb. 7th is Grant's birthday.
Feb. 14th is Valentine's Day.
Feb. 2nd is Groundhog Day.
Feb. 21st is Presidents' Day.
February is winter.
February is the shortest month.

The children have been taught that for questions labeled "Think," they should each decide on an answer to share at meeting instead of writing on the chart. In this case, where the answers would have been challenging for children to write by themselves, they brainstormed together, and Deborah wrote them during the meeting.

As students' reading skills improve, the amount of text in the message increases. Deborah continues to include the repeating sentences in each message. However, the focus is now on reading and talking about the nonrepeating sentences that follow.

Discussion during meeting helps the class prepare for the visit from the nurse, who will also use the information collected at the bottom of the chart in her presentation.

News and Announcements

Nathan is first, and Justin will turn out the lights. Today is Thursday, February 3^{rd,} 2005.

Nurse Wendy will visit our class today. She will talk about the food we need to be healthy and strong. What is one kind of food you think she will talk about?

Yesterday, did you eat:

fruit?	milk or cheese?	veggies?
Emily	Emily	Gus
		Emily
		Basil

News and Announcements

Grant is first, and Mimi will turn out the lights. Today is Monday, February 7th, 2005.

Ms. Porter will not be here today.
Ms. Howe and Ms. Geyster will be your teachers. What can you do to help?

Happy Birthday, Grant!

Practice the vowels:

a

e

i

o

u

By asking the children this question, Deborah reinforces the idea that they play a responsible role in this classroom community.

Straightforward, familiar skill practice can be a good choice for days when classroom routines are disrupted.

News and Announcements

Timmy is first, and Margaret will turn out the lights. Today is Tuesday, February 8th, 2005.

We have a new class pet. Do you know what it is? How will we care for it?

What do you think it eats?

plants	meat	both
✓ ✓ ✓ ✓ ✓		✓ ✓ ✓ ✓ ✓ ✓ ✓

Deciding on an answer for this specific question helps each child gather his or her ideas for the group discussion about how they might take care of a salamander.

News and Announcements

Emily is first, and Miles will turn out the lights. Today is Wednesday, February 9th, 2005.

Yesterday we found out our salamander is a meat eater. I found a caterpillar on the road. Do you think he would like it for breakfast?

More snow is coming!

Deborah follows through on a topic from the previous day. As the year progresses and students' reading skills improve, her sense of humor and personality become more evident in her messages.

Once students in this class had been formally introduced to letter-writing, Deborah began writing the message as a letter. During meeting, she helped the class, especially the kindergartners, notice that most of the words were the same.

Wednesday, February 16th, 2005

Dear Friends,

Today Grace is first, and Isabel will turn out the lights. We have gym today. I wonder what Mrs. Berger will have you play.

Regards,
Ms. Porter

Monday, February 28th, 2005

Dear Friends,

Today Mimi is first, and David will turn out the lights. Welcome back!

During vacation, Mr. Lively measured snow.

Saturday = 1 inch   Wednesday = 1 inch
Monday = 6 1/2 inches   Friday = 2 inches
Tuesday = 1/2 inch   Saturday = 1 inch

How can we figure out how much snow we got?

Regards,
Ms. Porter

Did you play in the snow on vacation?

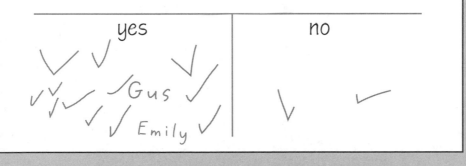

yes	no
✓ ✓ ✓ ✓ ✓ ✓ ✓ Gus ✓ ✓ ✓ Emily ✓	✓ ✓

Deborah continues to show the children that the new letter format is a predictable pattern, pointing out which familiar words appeared regularly in the same places.

The class would work together to add up the data collected by the school's custodian.

By connecting the topic of returning from vacation with the class's previous work on measuring snow, the message becomes a bridge from home to school.

Tuesday, March 8th, 2005

Dear Friends,

Today Isabel is first, and Nathan will turn out the lights.

The weather person said it would rain, rain, rain, and then snow, snow, snow!

Today we will learn more about how trees grow.

Best,
Ms. Porter

Draw a tree in winter:

Here Deborah uses the message to spark interest in an ongoing unit of study on trees. The children used their background knowledge to create a variety of drawings of what trees look like in winter, including different sizes and shapes of trees without leaves and some evergreens.

If time before morning meeting is limited, remember that drawing on the chart can be optional. Children could also keep adding drawings later or draw on separate pieces of paper or sticky notes.

Tuesday, March 22nd, 2005

Dear Friends,

Today Miles is first, and Timmy will turn out the lights.

Mr. Watt and I went scouting for owls. We heard one. It sounded like "Who cooks for you, who cooks for you all." Do you remember what kind that is?

Regards,
Ms. Porter

barred owl	great horned owl	screech owl
✓ ✓ ✓ ✓ ✓	✓ ✓ ✓	✓

The class is preparing for an "owl walk" in the woods, a special nighttime activity inspired by Jane Yolen's *Owl Moon*. Since they are likely to locate owls by hearing them, a naturalist who works with the school has been helping them learn to recognize the calls of different local owl species.

Students found consonant blends that make particular ending sounds in words in the message.

Dear Friends,

Today, Justin is first, and April will turn out the lights.

Ms. Porter is out. Ms. Geyster will be your teacher in the a.m. and Ms. *what's that?* Howe will be your teacher in the p.m. *what's that?*

We had hope on our owl walk, but no luck! We will try again at the full moon in May.

Regards,
Ms. Porter

Deborah uses the abbreviations "a.m." and "p.m." in the message for the first time. The familiar sentence structure and content provide context clues.

The words "hope" and "luck" echo language that the children heard in *Owl Moon*.

Thursday, March 31st, 2005

Dear Friends,

Today David is first, and Margaret will turn out the lights.

We keep thinking about what you told us about the problems on the bus. Do you think other kids in our school know how you feel? Should we tell them?

Your teachers,
Ms. Porter, Ms. Howe, Ms. Geyster

How do you get to school?

bus	car or van	walk
Emily Cody Jonah April Grant MILES	Mimi Basil Timmy Justin Nathan GRACE Isabel Gus	

Deborah writes this message after hearing from children that they feel scared of the older kids on the bus. By using "we" and including all the teachers' names, Deborah shows students that they are united in their concern. Conversation about this during meeting would be brief; if a longer discussion was needed, they'd come back to it in a separate class meeting later in the day.

The children's responses tell Deborah which students have firsthand experience with riding the bus. However, since the problems are affecting the whole community, the body of the message signals that everyone will be involved in problem-solving.

This message provides news about an ongoing topic of concern, but also names a fun learning activity the children can look forward to. Balancing serious and fun content helps children start the day feeling excited about what lies ahead.

Tuesday, April 5, 2005

Dear Friends,

Today Emily is first, and Mimi will turn out the lights.

How was the bus ride today? The older kids sent us a letter about the bus problems. Let's get together with them to talk about their idea.

The sun is finally out! Let's do some outdoor work this afternoon. How about a walk to the stream?

Regards,
Ms. Porter

Do you think there is snow in the woods?

yes	no

Monday, April 11, 2005

Dear Friends,

    Today Grant is first, and David will turn out the lights.

    How do you like our beautiful new rug? We need to send a thank-you to April's dad and granddad for putting it in. What could we make? Something yummy?

               Regards,

               Ms. Porter

Draw yourself on our new rug!

The rug in this classroom defines the space where the class gathers as a group for morning meeting and many other activities. Children drew themselves doing all sorts of things on their new rug and came to morning meeting with lots of ideas about how to thank April's father and grandfather.

This message gives the children a chance to begin thinking and talking about the shift to all-school lunch and recess. When they talked, Deborah tried to identify and resolve potential problems proactively. She also encouraged children to say what they were looking forward to about the new schedule.

Monday, April 25, 2005

Dear Friends,

Welcome back!

Today April is first, and Grace will turn out the lights.

Today we will begin to eat lunch and have recess with the whole school. Do you want help eating with the older kids?

We will begin a new afternoon schedule. After lunch and recess we will have quiet time and then read a story. After that everyone will do math together.

Yours,
Ms. Porter

Tuesday, April 26th, 2005

Dear Friends,

Today Justin is first, and Christian will turn out the lights.

It is spring! Yesterday we talked about how important the spring rain is. Today we will go outside and begin to explore how things are changing.

Best,
Ms. Porter

What do you think we will find?

Draw or write your idea:

Deborah designs tasks that can be completed quickly and confidently by children of varying reading and writing abilities. Here, "write or draw" allows the children to select the method that suits them.

The children drew trees with leaves, flowers, salamanders, insects, birds, and frogs. Children who didn't have a chance to draw or write before the meeting could share their ideas then and add to the chart later in the day.

Wednesday, April 27, 2005

Dear Friends,

Today Mimi is first, and David will turn out the lights.

Yesterday we saw many things in the woods. Some were in water, some were in air, and some were on land.

Draw or write something we saw yesterday in the woods:

The message reinforces and builds on what the class learned during their visit to the nearby woods. Deborah uses a diagram to organize the answers.

Monday, May 2, 2005

Dear Friends,

   Today Margaret is first, and Cody will turn out the lights. Ms. Geyster is sick. First graders will have a guest teacher.

   Last week we saw lots of things at the vernal pool. All the creatures are part of that habitat. Let's make a list of everything. Partners, help each other.

                                   Regards,
                                   Ms. Porter

What we saw at the vernal pool:
wood frog

sslaman   TATPOLW
wood frog   redbarys
salmandr   FROG EGGS
                        salomader eggs
MOSKEOLORVO   big blak betol
log   redberrys
   mistee goo

This message uses vocabulary that's related to the curriculum. Students have already been introduced to the words "vernal pool" and "habitat," so some will recognize these terms on their own, and everyone will understand them when the class reads the message together.

Tuesday, May 3rd, 2005

Dear Friends,

Today Christian is first, and Emily will turn out the lights.

We began a new month last Sunday. It is the month of <u>May</u> . Do you know of a holiday in May that we should remember?

Respectfully,
Ms. Porter

The closing can be a place to occasionally use an unfamiliar, challenging word. Students who can't read "respectfully" could still read the message, and the group would work together on decoding and defining the word during meeting.

Make "ay" words —
use b, d, g, h, j, l, m, p, r, s, w

gay

BAY
may
ray
PAY

day
lay
say

HAY
WAY
jay
GRAY
Play

Wednesday, May 4, 2005

Dear Scientists,

Today Timmy is first, and Jonah will turn out the lights.

Yesterday I brought in some water from a vernal pool. I saw that all the wood frog eggs had hatched, but the salamander eggs had not. I wonder why? Today we will be scientists and study the water.

Regards,
Ms. Porter

Deborah chooses a greeting related to the topic of the message. This greeting reinforces their image of themselves as scientists.

Keep in mind that messages can invite student participation without requiring a written response. In this message, the children are invited to participate by wondering along with Deborah and making hypotheses which they will talk about at meeting or during science time.

Monday, May 9th, 2005

Dear Sons and Daughters,

Today Gus is first, and April will turn out the lights.

How did your moms like the pots and plants? Did you do something special for Mother's Day?

This week we will begin to learn about shapes. Shapes are everywhere!

Affectionately,
Ms. Porter

Draw a shape you like:

The children drew squares, ovals, circles, triangles, stars, and a heart. This task is designed to generate enthusiasm for a new unit of study about shapes.

Tuesday, May 10th, 2005

Dear Friends,

Today Grace is first, and Isabel will turn out the lights. Ms. Howe is sick.

Yesterday we learned that the word (geometry) is a fancy word for studying about shapes. We will use shapes to make pictures today.

Regards,
Ms. Porter

Color 1/2 a shape to make a new one.

When Deborah uses this relatively new vocabulary word in the message, she emphasizes it visually and includes a reminder about its definition in the text.

During meeting or a math lesson, the class might work on naming the original shapes and the shapes they made by coloring.

Wednesday, May 11th, 2005

Dear Friends,

Today is a 1/2 day. David is first, and Basil will turn out the lights.

This morning we will all work together on reading and writing. What book will you read? Do you think other kids would enjoy it?

Regards,
Ms. Porter

Check the books you have read.

Hop on Pop	Go Dog Go	Pot of Gold	Magic Tree House	Green Eggs and Ham

This task may help students get ideas about the book they'll choose to read later in the day. For many children, having a few titles to choose among can be more manageable than being given a larger selection.

Thursday, May 12ᵗʰ, 2005

Dear Friends,

Today Jonah is first, and Gus will turn out the lights.

Did you see how the tadpoles and eggs are changing? Do you think the vernal pool is changing, too?

Regards,
Ms. Porter

Draw a tree in spring:

On a previous chart the children drew trees in winter. Now the class might compare those drawings with the ones they make today and talk about the differences they notice.

Friday, May 13, 2005

Dear Friends,

    Ms. Howe is back! The sun is out! What a way to start a day. Alexander will be first, and Isabel will turn out the lights.

    We have 2 vernal pool pictures left to do: the winter and the fall. What colors will we need to use?

                        Regards,
                        Ms. Porter

Deborah continues to include the predictable pattern of sentences in the message every day, but as the children's confidence about reading increases, she sometimes varies their placement and wording.

Monday, May 16ᵗʰ, 2005

Dear Scientists,

Today Emily is first, and Miles will turn out the lights.

We have learned so much about vernal pools. I think we should write a book about them. What will we include?

Regards,
Ms. Porter

Can you hear peepers at your house?

yes	?	no
Ms. Porter MILES Mimi Emily Jonah Timmy Justin Nathan April	Basil Gus Cody	Grant GRACE Isabel

When Deborah uses the message to celebrate how much the children have learned, their awareness of their accomplishments grows.

Peepers are tree frogs with a distinctive call that's heard in the spring. The children who added an "I don't know" category were not sure what a peeper sounded like, so they could not answer "yes" or "no." Their impromptu revision shows their comfort admitting that they did not know and that they wanted to make the chart include their experience.

Tuesday, May 17th, 2005

Dear Friends,

Today Miles is first, and Grant will turn out the lights.

Yesterday we made a great start to our vernal pool book. Today we will plan the rest of the pages. Vernal pools are a great way to study the seasons. Why do you think that is?

The older children in our school will be working hard on MCAS testing today. How can we help them?

Regards,
Ms. Porter

At the beginning of a period of standardized testing, Deborah encourages students to think of themselves as supportive members of their school community. At meeting she'd ask students to share ideas about how they can help the older students.

Monday, May 23, 2005

Dear Friends,

Today Nathan is first, and Gus will turn out the lights.

Today we will start building our block town. At meeting you can think about the building you want to make. I'll choose partners. You get to choose what you build.

Regards,
Ms. Porter

A bubble in a corner is a good way to include last minute news. Putting such news outside the body of message allows you to maintain the focus you have selected for the day.

Tuesday, May 24th, 2005

Dear Builders,

Another rainy day, but we have the gym for recess! Timmy is first, and Basil will turn out the lights.

Our block town really looks like a town! Today we will work on the insides of the buildings. What kinds of things would people who work in your building need to do their jobs?

Regards,
Ms. Porter

By the end of the year, Deborah's messages have become much lengthier and have a more conversational tone. Comparing charts from the beginning of the year with later ones can help the children see how much their reading has improved.

Tuesday, May 31st, 2005

Dear Writers,

    I hope everyone had a great weekend! Today Jonah is first, and Mimi will turn out the lights.

    We need to finish the words for our book. What will happen in the summer and fall at the vernal pool?

                    Regards,
                    Ms. Porter

Draw or write something you saw in the vernal pool last week.

The children drew and wrote about frogs, sala-manders, egg masses, and insects, among other things.

Dear Friends,

Goodbye, May! Hello, June! Today Emily is first, and Justin will turn out the lights.

Are there any holidays in June? Who has a birthday in June?

Cody   Justin

How are you doing on your building? What did you work on yesterday? Today let's try to finish the building.

Regards,
Ms. Porter

Although Deborah has observed the progress of the multi-day building project, by asking students to assess and report on whether their work is complete, she reinforces their sense of themselves as independent and capable workers.

Is your building done?

yes	no
Nathan MILES Grant Emily Gus April Jonah GRACE Justin Timmy Cody	Mimi Basil Isabel

Monday, June 6th, 2005

Dear Friends,

Today Grace is first, and Cody will turn out the lights.

The block town looks almost finished. Do you have anything you need to do to your building?

We have 3 more weeks of school and 4 important things to accomplish:

1. Vernal Pool/Community Project
2. Practice
3. Write a report card about the year
4. Have fun together

Regards,
Ms. Porter

During meeting Deborah and the class talk about what each of the four things on the list means, and what it means to "accomplish" them.

The concept of "practice" is already familiar to the children, but now the reason for practice is expressed as getting skills "locked in their heads" so they can use them during the summer.

Tuesday, June 7th, 2005

Dear Friends,

Today Mimi is first, and Cody will turn out the lights. The preschool will eat lunch with us today at 11:30. You will help them learn about eating in the cafeteria.

Remember our 4 end-of-the-year jobs? Today we will have fun and practice math!

Regards,
Ms. Porter

Fill in:

1 2 3 4 5 6 7 8 9 10
11 12 13 14 15 16 17 18 19 20
21 22 23 24 25

Wednesday, June 8ᵗʰ, 2005

Dear Friends,

    Today is a half day. Justin is first, and Grant will turn out the lights.

    How is the play going in the block town? I noticed that the road was not sturdy. I also noticed kids fixing it. That is just what a road crew would do.

               Best,
               Ms. Porter

Here, Deborah uses the message to describe specific positive behavior she noticed in the block area. By directing her comments to the whole class, she invites them all to consider what it means to be "like a road crew" and to think of other things that people might do to care for a town.

Monday, June 13th, 2005

Dear Friends,

Today Emily is first, and Grace will turn out the lights. It will be hot again today.

This week is a special project week. Every class in the school will be working on a project. We will make a model of the vernal pool for our project. What will we need to put in the model? Mr. Watt will help us get started.

We will get to be together all week!

Best,
Ms. Porter

The message and morning meeting provide structure for the class during a week of intensive project-based learning together, with no pull-outs for instruction. The familiar routines help the children and Deborah connect, plan, and reflect as they begin each day.

Wednesday, June 15, 2005

Dear Researchers,

Gus is first, and David will turn out the lights.

We got lots done on our model yesterday. I was surprised at how many circles of life there are in a vernal pool.

Today we will keep working on the background and do some research about the animals.

Regards,
Ms. Porter

Before meeting, make 5 leaves for the model. Bring them to meeting.

Deborah uses the greeting to indicate the type of work the children will be doing on the class project that day. Addressing the students as "Researchers" emphasizes that she sees this as important, grown-up work, which is appealing to children.

Thursday, June 16th, 2005

Dear Scientists,

Today we will work on our model. How do you like the green leaves?

We need to draw the animals today. I don't know how we can make them move, but I have an idea about how we can make them look like they are under water.

Regards,
Ms. Porter

Ms. Porter is first. Mr. Watt will turn out the lights!

The day before, the class decided they wanted the animals in the model to move just as they do in the water. In her response to this idea, Deborah models the sort of problem-solving style she wants the class to use.

On a particularly unpredictable, jam-packed day, it can be challenging for students to do these jobs, so Deborah playfully appoints herself and the naturalist to do them.

Tuesday, June 21st, 2005

Dear Friends,

    This is the longest day of the year! Isabel is first, and David will turn out the lights.

    Today we will finish up our end-of-the-year reports. What do you think was the most important thing you learned this year?

                 Regards,
                 Ms. Porter

What fun Field Day was yesterday! Draw yourself at Field Day!

During the final days of school, the consistent format and reassuring content of the message can help students stay focused as they review the year and celebrate their accomplishments.

The children drew themselves playing at the school's recent Field Day. Many students feel sad at the end of the school year. This activity helps children begin the day by remembering something positive and enjoyable.

Good Morning, C___

This afternoo___
Spring Sho___
are you look___

We will ___
audience s___
show. Thi___
to show ___
to share ___

Good Morning, Chilly___

It is another cold___
my house this morn___

At 2:45 we will h___
to see our Shared___
song, "A Gift of So___

What question___
read the words t___

? Why did the scarf___
white? S.O.
? ¿Porque ella no po___
hablar?
? Why did Maya___
bird to be blue?___
? Why did the bl___
sing?

January 27, 2005

October 25 , 2004

Dear Readers,

This week we have been
reading <u>Touch the Earth</u> together.

How do you touch the earth?

By touching the flowers DH
by working on the
grass BO
by the sun
coming out DH
I plant a garden SO
I touch the earth by singing OM
Plant some plants XM
By swimming
at the beach DG
By touching the sand NC

Messages from a
3rd Grade
Classroom

ROSALEA S. FISHER

September __20__ , __2004__

Dear Third Graders,

   We have learned a lot about each other over the past few weeks. Today we'll use some of what we've learned to play a game. Help us learn more by answering this question:

What is something you do really well?

[Mrs. F.] I can make quilts. [ ]

[O.M.] I can make quesadillas. [SO] I can do the monkey Bars Backwords

[FL] I can make pictures. [NC] I can jump rope with a hula hoop.

[JS] I can goob to do pictures. [XM] I can Read hula

[ ] [CP] I can jo ff good

[D.M] I can make pictures. [DG] I Can do Math good

Messages from a Third Grade Bilingual Classroom

ROSALEA S. FISHER

3rd grade teacher, K.T. Murphy Elementary School, Stamford, Connecticut

EVERY MORNING the first thing I do when I come into my classroom is go to the easel and write the day's morning meeting message chart. This is my moment to welcome the students, set the tone for our day together, and spark students' interest in the learning we'll be doing. Just as students look forward to morning meeting as a way to start their day of learning, I rely on writing the message as a way to launch my day of teaching.

Even though each day's message is different, it usually only takes me a few minutes to write it. This is because I plan what I will say ahead of time; by the time I walk in the door I've already decided what to focus on for that day. To decide, I think about the academic and social learning we're doing at the moment and what aspect is important enough to feature in the message. I also think about what mood I want the message to have. The nature of each day is different: Sometimes the mood is lighter; sometimes it's more serious. This thinking takes time, although I can do it more quickly now than when I started.

I am always looking for ways to bring academics in. I'll use the message to ask the children what they know about a topic such as Native Americans or multiplication, and then use their responses to lead into a new unit of study or to review the previ-

ous day's lesson. Answers to a question like "What did you do during your vacation?" might provide data we'll use to make a graph during math. A question like "What is the big problem in the story you are writing?" can launch a rich discussion about the writing process.

I also use the charts to prompt children to reflect on how they worked on a project or how an activity went. Messages sometimes help us prepare for events, from field trips to testing. At the end of the year, messages launch discussions about moving on to fourth grade.

Whatever the content of the message charts, they give the children important practice in literacy. So much of what we do in third grade is based on reading, and the message gives students a chance to practice every day with text that was written just for them. As the year progresses and the needs of the children change, the message changes, too. At the beginning of the year when we focus on letter writing, the message is a daily model. In the middle of the year, after we've accumulated lots of words on our class Word Wall, those words appear in the charts frequently. At the end of the year, sentences in the message become more complex and vocabulary is more challenging. Also, when we work on editing, I include more punctuation errors and misspellings for them to find.

We read and talk about the message for a few minutes at the end of morning meeting, often just touching on topics we'll return to later in the day. In this way, the message chart serves as a bridge from morning meeting to the day's academic work. It's an indispensable part of the school day.

School and Classroom Demographics

K.T. Murphy Elementary School is in Stamford, a small city on the coast of Connecticut. Stamford is a very diverse community. Dozens of languages are spoken here, and residents have a wide range of incomes.

The school has over 500 students in grades K–5. Most of them come from the working class neighborhood near the school. Many of K.T. Murphy's students are Latino; some are recent immigrants and others are the children of immigrants. About half of the students at K.T. Murphy qualify for free or reduced price lunch.

K.T. Murphy has made the *Responsive Classroom* approach a school-wide initiative, and all the teachers and many other adults in the building have been trained in the components of the approach. Every class in the school has morning meeting every day.

The morning message charts in this section were made for a bilingual class of twenty-two third graders. All but six of the students were bilingual or English language learners. Most came from Spanish-speaking countries, but there were also a few from Bangladesh and the Ukraine. One child had just come from South America and knew very little English. There were thirteen boys and nine girls in the class.

At K.T. Murphy, most bilingual classrooms have two full-time certified teachers. That year my co-teacher was Alix Meza, a native Spanish speaker. Since bilingual education in Stamford focuses on teaching students to use English (as opposed to the "two way" approach some schools use, where students learn in two languages), we do not provide formal instruction in Spanish. Throughout the year Alix worked closely with our Spanish-speaking students, providing support and encouraging them to use English more and more over the course of the year. Otherwise, we shared responsibility for most of what took place in the classroom, including leading morning meeting. However, I always wrote the day's message on the chart.

The Children's Academic and Social Skills

When this group of students arrived in the fall, their English oral language skills were not as strong as they needed to be. Their reading comprehension was weak, and their spelling was even weaker. Since English was a second language for so many of them, this was not a surprise. As the year progressed, many of them improved their reading and writing skills, and some became accomplished readers. Their favorite subject was math. They were all willing to learn and wanted to be strong students.

Early on their social skills were much stronger than their academic skills. Many of them had been at K.T. Murphy since kindergarten and were familiar with morning meeting, the rule-making process, and other components of the *Responsive Classroom* approach. Still, knowing and living by the rules was sometimes a problem for this class. Alix and I addressed this with a lot of proactive reminding and spent a fair amount of time leading the class in reflecting on "how it went," when the "it" was a day with a guest teacher, a lesson, a trip, or recess. When I used the morning message to initiate reflection, I would first note what the children had done well, and then follow with discussion about what could have gone better.

Morning meeting and the message were an important part of the day for this class. Some children would always go right to the message as soon as they arrived, before they did the rest of their morning check-ins. More of them might have, except that some children rode busses that consistently arrived late. Those children usually would not have time to focus on the chart until we read it together at the end of morning meeting. We always read the chart together chorally because reading aloud is such good fluency practice for English language learners.

The boy who'd just come from South America loved writing on the chart. He really wanted to know what the message said and used the skills he was learning to figure it out. He picked up English quickly, and I know the charts helped him.

My Teaching Style

I have been an elementary school teacher for more than twenty-five years. I began my career teaching second grade and have taught fourth and fifth as well, but I have taught third grade most, and it is my favorite.

I want children to have authentic tasks that support their learning. I also work hard to help children become their own problem solvers. I teach them to work through tasks step-by-step, and give them lots of opportunities to practice. Then, when they are ready, I love to send them off to make choices and work independently. Giving children choices in their learning is what gives me the greatest joy.

To achieve the authentic learning that I value, I spend a lot of time creating tasks and activities rather than lifting them from books. It keeps my creative juices flowing and makes learning more fun for students.

The *Responsive Classroom* approach and morning meeting in particular fit my personal teaching philosophy well. Morning meeting messages, a key element of the *Responsive Classroom* approach, have grown to be a critical part of my teaching practice.

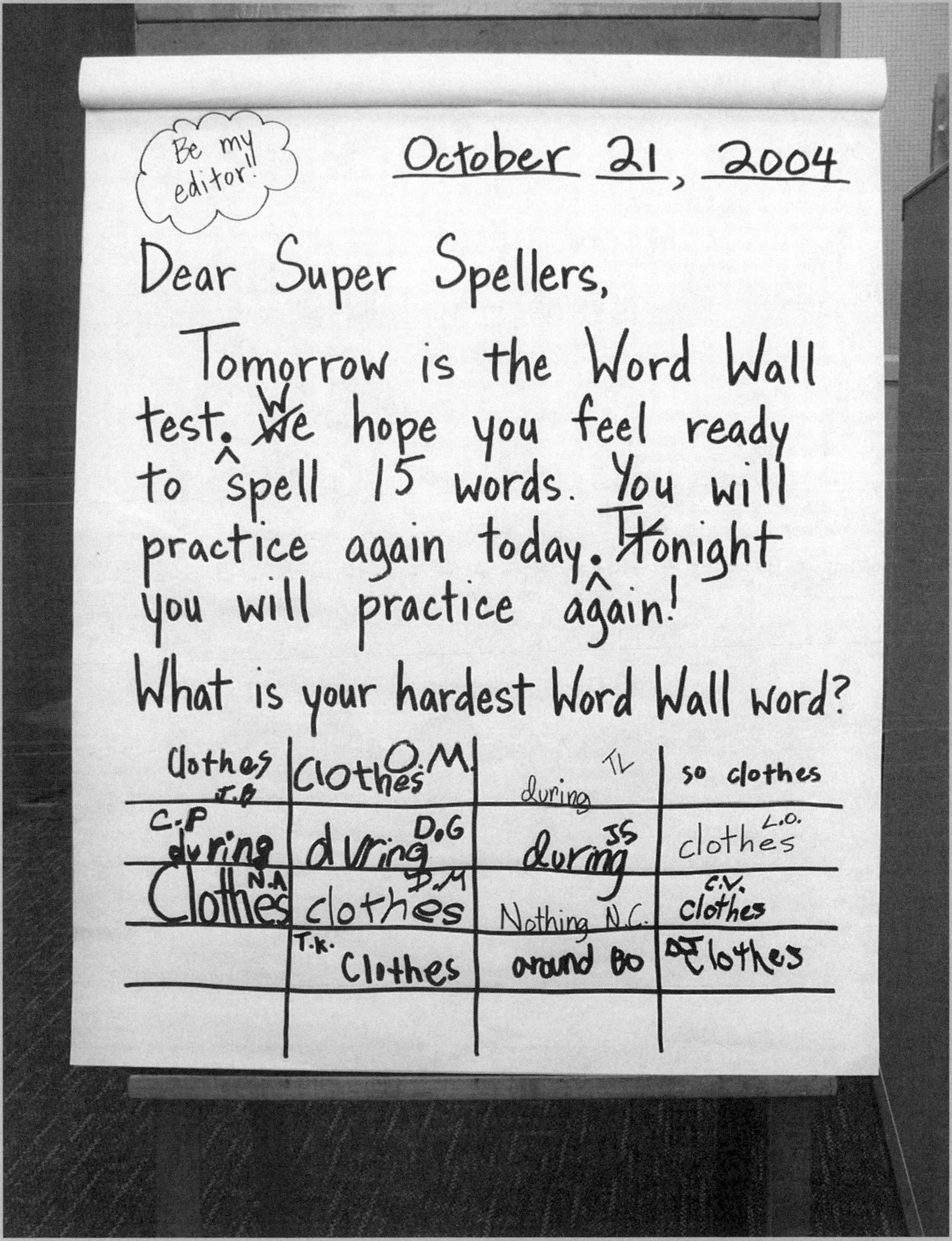
Be my editor!
October 21, 2004
Dear Super Spellers,
Tomorrow is the Word Wall test. We hope you feel ready to spell 15 words. You will practice again today. Tonight you will practice again!
What is your hardest Word Wall word?
Clothes T.B.
Clothes O.M.
during TL
so clothes
C.P during
during D.G
during JS
clothes L.O.
Clothes N.A
clothes D.M
Nothing N.C.
C.V. clothes
T.K. Clothes
around BO
DJ Clothes

At the beginning of the year, it's important to teach students how to work with the message. For example, after the class reads this message together, Rosalea would explain that there would be a new message for them to read at the beginning of each day.

Then the class might talk about ways to make sure everyone has a chance to read the chart. They might practice skills such as turn-taking, standing without blocking others' view, and waiting a bit if there's a crowd at the chart.

August 30, 2004

Good Morning!
   Welcome to third grade.
Welcome to Room 21.
   We will spend a lot of time in the days ahead getting to know each other.

Buenos Días!
   Bienvenidos al tercer grado.
Bienvenidos al salón 21.
   Durante la semana tendremos mucho tiempo para conocerenos mejor.

On the first day of school, writing the message in English and Spanish for this bilingual class clearly signals that everyone belongs in this classroom community.

September 2, 2004

Dear Third Graders,

Yesterday I noticed how carefully you listened to your teachers and to each other. Let's try to do the same today!

Ayer note que bien escucharon a sus maestros y a sus amigos. Intentaremeos hacer lo mismo hoy.

Cuál fue tu mejor momento este verano?
What was your best moment this summer?

✓my brother came   ✓swimming
✓I went to Tennessee   ✓My friends
✓Niagara Falls   ✓
✓camping   ✓Playing at the beach
✓My dad played with me ✓Going to Playland
✓Six Flags   ✓I played with my sister

Since most of the students in this class had worked with morning messages before and had experience responding to tasks on the chart, Rosalea was able to include tasks in her messages early in the year.

The checkmarks guide students on how much to write. This can be helpful at the beginning of the year.

Regardless of the children's previous experience, when tasks start appearing on message charts it's important to go over the skills they need to manage them successfully, such as deciding what to write before taking a marker.

The message does not have to ask for a written response. "Thinking" questions may be introduced when students are able to think through their ideas independently and can choose one to share.

September 3, 2004

Dear Math Thinkers,

Today is our first math warm-up test. We will also have a Minute Math test. Think about the math strategies we have practiced this week. Be ready to share one strategy you remember during morning meeting.

In this bilingual class, the goal for all students was to improve their skills in English. Because the daily message provided a high interest opportunity for students to practice reading in English, the message was translated for the first few days of school, and then written mostly in English for the rest of the year.

September 8, 2004 — date

salutation

Dear Students,

indent | We will learn how to buzz today. It's a lot of fun. It is a time to talk about books.

indent | Today we will also write letters to our parents. We will display them for Open House.

indent | What ideas should we put in our letters to parents?

Sincerely, — closing
Mrs. Fisher — signature

Here, the message chart becomes a real-life example for the class as they learn about letter-writing. By labeling the parts of a letter in the message during morning meeting, Rosalea reinforces vocabulary and what the children are learning about letter format.

Although she doesn't usually sign her messages, Rosalea includes a closing and signature because the class is learning about letter format.

Using a signal such as a bubble at the bottom of the chart helps students know whether they should respond to a question in writing. (See Sept. 2 message for an example). Since there is no bubble on this chart, students know that a written response is not expected.

Some teachers select a student to fill in any blanks in the message, either before or during morning meeting. Others have the group decide during morning meeting.

When an individual student is given responsibility for filling in a blank, it can be helpful to check the answer before it's written on the chart. This ensures that the student experiences success and that the message is a model of good writing for the rest of the class.

September <u>9</u>, 2004

Dear Letter Writers,

This morning you will finish your letters to your parents. Mrs. Meza and I hope to see many parents tonight.

Which greeting should Mrs. Meza and I do tonight with your parents?

(DT) Math facts   (CV) Hickety-Pickety   (DH) Math facts

(LO) Squeeze   ( )   ( )

( )   (TL) foreign language   ( )

(NA) Squeeze   (DJ) Squeeze   ( )

September 13, 2004

Good Morning!

   We will do homework in school this afternoon. What helps you to do homework well? Be ready to share your ideas in our meeting.

Morning meeting messages can address one idea very simply. They don't need to be creative, cute, or funny. Simple authenticity can be very effective at sparking students' thinking.

To prepare students to do homework successfully at home, Rosalea and Alix had them practice first by doing "homework in school." The process started with discussion at this morning meeting.

In cases like this, many teachers will write the brainstormed ideas on the chart so the class can refer to them later.

This bubble alerts students that recess will be held indoors. Using just a few words and establishing a corner of the message for such notices emphasizes that they are important, but not part of the regular message.

After deciding on their individual hopes and dreams for the year, this class developed classroom rules that would help all the students accomplish their goals.

Structured Play—Indoors

September 17, 2004

Dear Rule Makers,

We have done a lot of important thinking and talking together about our rules.

Today we will create a bulletin board to display our rules. How can we make our bulletin board beautiful? Be ready to share an idea about this at our morning meeting.

September <u>20</u>, <u>2004</u>

Dear Third Graders,

We have learned a lot about each other over the past few weeks. Today we'll use some of what we've learned to play a game.

Help us learn more by answering this question:

What is something you do really well?

Mrs. F | I can make quilts. [ ]

O.M. | I can make quesadillas   S.O. | I can do the monkey bars backwards

D.M. | I can make pictures.   NC | I can jump rope with a hula hoop.

T.L. | I can make pictures.   C.P. | I can jump good

[ ]   D.G. | I can do math good

In this class, the message was read chorally, with one child pointing to each word before it was read. Children usually read their own responses aloud. This practice was especially helpful to the English language learners.

Other teachers vary how the charts are read, sometimes having the class read in unison, and sometimes having partners, groups ("everyone wearing stripes" for example), or individuals read different sections. Varying the routine can help maintain students' interest.

At the beginning of the year, questions that help students get to know each other can work well because they are interesting and usually easy to answer.

Rather than making the whole group wait while one child decides what to write, you can engage everyone in thinking about what to write in the blanks in the message. Once the group decides, one or two students can quickly do the writing on the chart.

September 22, 2004

Dear Hardworking Students,

   Today is the first day of fall. Another word for fall is autumn. At 12:30 p.m., autumn will arrive. Today there will be darkness outside for the same length of time as there is light.

What is your favorite season?

Mrs. Meza			DJ
JB	NC	CP	NC
TK	OM	TK	DJ
OM	DO	JB	DG
DG	BO	AA	DM
OM	Mrs. Fisher	DG	CA
Fall 6	Winter 5	Spring 5	Summer 6

Introduce new task formats to students before asking them to work independently. In this case, you could tell students to wait until the meeting to complete the graph. During meeting, a few students could demonstrate filling in their initials. The rest could respond later in the day.

September 27, 2004

Dear Poetry Readers,

   We have been studying the poem "Sounds of Winter." What are some sounds YOU hear during winter? What about in autumn or other seasons? Get ready to share your ideas at morning meeting.

   What is your favorite line from "Sounds of Winter"?

- Nesting in trees forty feet tall
- Dark December Dinosaurs
- When ogres go and winter comes
- The fee-fie-foes and dreadful fums.
- Fee-fi-foor fom
- Dark December Dinosaurs
- Dark December Dinosaurs
- "When Ogres go and winter comes."
- Of Dark December Dinosaurs

Some teachers also include the day of the week in the date, especially if that information is not written elsewhere in the classroom.

In this class, there sometimes wasn't enough time for every student to respond in writing before the meeting. It's not necessary to have full written participation on the message each day, as long as over time all students participate frequently.

At the beginning of a new month, Rosalea writes the name of the month so that when children first encounter the word it is legible and spelled correctly.

October 4, 2004

Good Morning, Readers.

Today we will talk about our library. You will choose five books to keep in your blue bag. You will also read silently.

What kind of books do you like to read?

During meeting or later in the day, the class might use this list to get ideas about types of books they'd like to try, or to begin a discussion of fiction/nonfiction.

books about people - Mrs. F.   Dr. Seuss - XM

poetry   Martin's books - OM   science

chapter books - DH

history books   music   picture book

picture books   chapter books

Derek Jeter- SO   Miss Nelson - DT

sports

After students have practiced fitting their writing into designated spaces for a while, using big open bubbles allows them to practice judging how much space they need and simplifies chart preparation.

October 12, 2004

D ear Minute Math Thinkers,

   We will have our Minute Math test today. What strategies do you use when you do Minute Math?

count with my hands

count in my head

I use my brain

I start with the bigger number

I count with my fingers

One way to expand on responses like these is to ask students to show how they'd use their strategies on a sample problem. Have other students use a "thumbs up" or other "me, too" signal to show that they use the same strategies. Students might also keep adding to the list after the meeting.

This bubble alerts the children to a special event. By the time the class reads the chart together at the end of the meeting, the visitors will have come and gone. Therefore, it's important to keep the body of the message focused on something students will be doing later in the day.

This class created a guide to introduce substitute teachers ("guest teachers") to their classroom rules and routines.

Mrs. Taliercio's class will teach us a song in MM

October 13, 2004

Good Morning, Letter Writers.

Today we will write one more letter for our Guest Teacher Handbook. It will be a letter of introduction.

What do you think we should write about in a letter introducing our Guest Teacher Handbook?

If time allowed, the class might talk briefly about this question during meeting, or Rosalea might simply ask them to think about it until later when they work on the letter.

<u>October 19</u> , <u>2004</u>

Dear Good Listeners,

    We will continue our work with sound words this morning. Think of sounds you have heard. What words could you use to describe those sounds? Get ready to share your ideas.

    Write an animal sound.

Splat!   Woof

Moo   Onk onk onk   Zzzzz

Moo   ¡Miu!

¡Pio!   Cuac

Tweet

Teachers sometimes feel pressured to come up with different "fun" greetings, but it's fine to use simple, straight-forward greetings most of the time. Customized greetings should use words that relate to the topic of the message as "listeners" does here.

This simple activity provides a confidence-building warm-up for thinking about the more challenging question posed in the body of the message.

By this time, students had begun learning about editing and proofreading. Now, Rosalea teaches them to recognize this note as a cue to look for errors she has deliberately made in the message.

Including deliberate errors allows students to practice identifying and correcting mistakes. Each student thinks on his or her own, and then during morning meeting the class agrees upon the corrections before writing them on the chart.

October 21, 2004

Dear Super Spellers,

Tomorrow is the Word Wall test, we hope you feel ready to spell 15 words. You will practice again today, tonight you will practice again!

What is your hardest Word Wall word?

clothes J.B.	during C.P.		clothes N. A.
clothes O.M.	clothes D.M.	clothes T.K.	
during TL		during JS	nothing N.C.
	around B.O.		

Keep in mind that editing tasks on the chart should be a review, not a new lesson. In this case, the class had already learned to recognize run-on sentences and to use editing marks to correct them.

October 25, 2004

Dear Readers,

This week we have been reading <u>Touch the Earth</u> together.

How do you touch the earth?

By touching the flowers DH

by working on the grass BO

by the sun coming out DJ

I plant a garden SO

I touch the earth by singing OM

Plant some plants XM

By swimming at the beach DG

By touching the sand NC

Questions that invite children's creativity usually elicit enthusiastic responses. This message helps students connect literature study with personal experience in a simple, effective way.

November 1, 2004

Good Morning, <u>Writers.</u>

    We have been practicing letter writing for a few weeks. Today you will work independently to write a letter to Mr. Lewis, our librarian.

    What's the hardest part about writing a letter for you?

Write what I like

Periods and capitals

What to write about

What to write about

the body

to make my ideas very clear

With questions that ask students to share weaknesses, teachers generally bring the discussion during morning meeting around to positive, proactive strategies. In this case, the class might brainstorm about strategies they could use to improve or to help each other.

Be my editor!

November 4, 2004

Dear Students,

We have been learning about César Chávez. We Will continue today.

Write one thing you remember about César Chávez.

1. César Chávez no comió por 25 días. DT
2. that people laughed when he talked SO
3. César Chávez lived on a farm. OM
4. He went from place to place DM
5. El quería hacer justicia para los campesinos
6. that he did not eat JB
7.
8.
9.
10.

Asking students what they remember about a topic provides them with a chance to review. It can also give the teacher a sense of what they've understood.

Spelling and grammar mistakes made by students on tasks are usually not a focus of attention during morning meeting. However, when student responses are unclear, such as "that he did not eat," ask the student to explain what she or he meant.

This message creates an opportunity for exploring the meaning of the word "veteran." Since it's likely that some students will not know what a veteran is until the meeting, a word-find task is a good choice because students can complete it successfully without knowing the meaning of the word.

Some teachers use "no repeats" when they want to stretch students' thinking and are confident that the students have the skills they need to do independent work.

November <u>8, 2004</u>

Dear Paraders,

Yesterday many of you marched in the Veterans Day parade. You honored the men and women who have protected our country. What's one thing you will remember about the parade? Be ready to share it at our meeting.

What's one word you can make from the letters of the word "veteran"? (No repeats.)

tear CF	vet CP	
tea OM	ran TK	
never ED	enter XM	
rent TL	even LO	
van DG		

<u>November 18, 2004</u>

Good Morning, Readers!

We will read a book called <u>The Place I Love</u> today. It's about a boy who lives in the country.

What is your favorite place?

Mexico DG

my blue chair—Mrs. Fisher

Florida ED

Disney World JS

California DT

my school DM

Playland DH

Florida LO

my country CF

My favorite place is my country TK

Tennessee TL

Florida SO

Orlando O.M.

My favorite place is the school CV

my country PM

When the goal of the message is to get students excited about something new, Rosalea asks a question that they can respond to with just a few words. This cuts down on the amount of time each student needs for writing and maximizes the total number of responses.

Student responses create an opportunity to talk about the different meanings of "country."

This chart shows how words embedded in the message can be used to practice a spelling skill. Rosalea deliberately includes /-ing/ words in the message and then asks students to find those with base words that don't change. Those words are circled and their base words are underlined.

The activity was extended by identifying /-ing/ words in the chart that did not follow the pattern, and writing their base words.

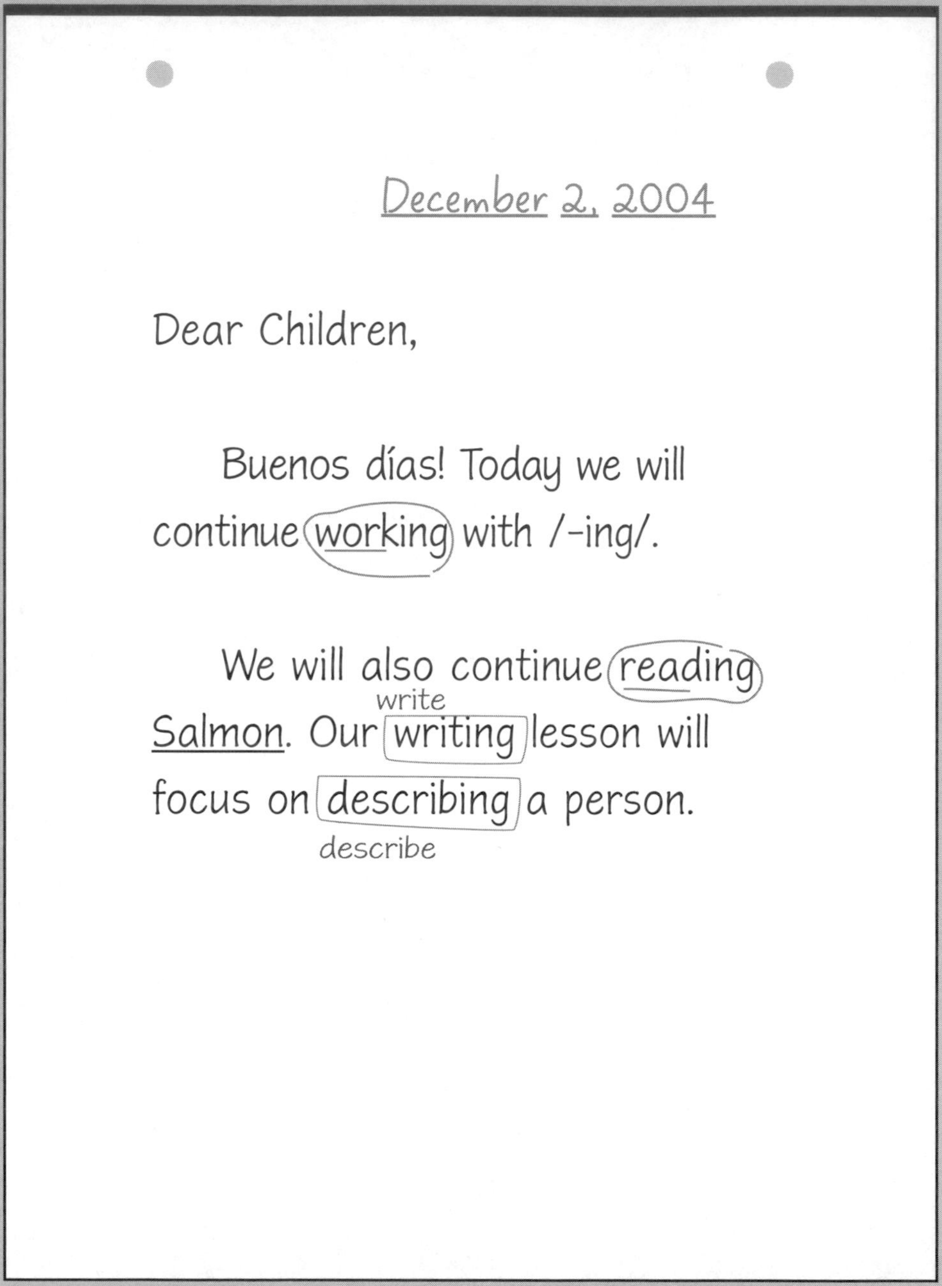

December 2, 2004

Dear Children,

Buenos días! Today we will continue (working) with /-ing/.

We will also continue (reading)
write
Salmon. Our [writing] lesson will focus on [describing] a person.
describe

<u>December 3, 2004</u>

Dear Salmon Researchers,

At 12:00 we will play WORDO with our Word Wall words. It's a great way to practice them.

We will also read more about salmon today.

What do you know so far about salmon?

They swim up stream. S.O.		The Atlantic salmon may live 10 years. C.P.
Salmon lay 8000 eggs. C.V.	Que los salmones Chum y Rosado viven en el océano Pácifico del Norte. E.M.	They are 8 different types of salmons.
Only Atlantic salmon live in the Atlantic ocean.		There is 1 type of salmon in the Pacific Ocean and in the Atlantic there are 7 types of salmons. OM
They go back to where they were born to lay their eggs. N.C.	That Atlantic salmon makes his nest with his tail.	

Since responding to this question requires a good deal of writing, students might need to begin before meeting and continue adding to the chart afterwards. Another way to make long responses manageable is to give each student a sticky note to write on.

Student responses that are unclear can reinforce misinformation, so it is important to ask students what they meant when they seem to have their facts wrong. When possible, help them clarify what they wrote.

Try to have students do more with responses than just read back what they wrote. To encourage higher level thinking in this case you might ask "What are you hoping you will find out about salmon?" or "Using what's written here, can you summarize what we know about salmon so far?"

Putting the guest teacher's name in the chart includes her in the class's routines. In this case, writing her name in the message during meeting helps the class remember it. You could also put the guest teacher's name in a corner bubble.

Using a "What do you know?" question to begin a unit of study can help students feel less intimidated about learning something new. Seeing the list of responses tells the class that they are not starting from scratch; they already know some things about the new subject.

<u>December 6, 2004</u>

Hola, Niños!

Mrs. Meza is absent today. Our guest teacher is <u>Miss Desronvil</u>.

We will begin to learn about multiplication today. What do you know about multiplication already?

that when you put $1 \times 1 = 1$	that $2 \times 3 = 6$	That $2 \times 2 = 4$ like $2 + 2 = 4$
that $1 \times 2 = 2$	that $5 \times 5 = 25$	
$1 + 1 = 2$	I know $1 \times 3 = 3$	I know $2 \times 2 = 4$
$1 \times 2 = 2$	that $6 \times 3 = 18$	

<u>December 17, 2004</u>

Good Morning, Everyone.

We will finish our holiday cards this morning. Let's decorate them with sparkles!

Are you ready for our Word Wall test?

How did you practice last night?

Con las cartas que yo hice el martes. E.M.	
I practiced by my Dad saying the words	I wrote sentences C.P.
by alphabetic order S.O.	
By the hardest words J.B	I practiced by doing main ideas. T.K.
Las practiqué repitiendo y repitiendo C.A	I practiced by writing on the paper.
	I practiced doing questions.

This type of question encourages students to share strategies. Discussion during the meeting could include further explanation of particular strategies, giving examples, and asking "Who else uses this strategy?"

A follow-up question for a check-in or the next day's meeting might be "Did your strategy help? Will you do anything differently next time?"

As the year goes on, some teachers give students responsibility for selecting the greeting that starts their morning meeting. If you have students choose greetings, it's important to have a system that allows every child to have a turn.

This message helps students reconnect with classroom routines and expectations after time away from school. The content and tone remind the children: "You are competent and trustworthy, and you have important responsibilities as a member of our community."

Today's greeting: Nina

January 3, 2005!

Dear Third Graders,

It's a new year. It's a new month. That means new jobs and new seats. What is your new job for January? Please check the chart to see how you will be helping this month.

January 4, 2005

Good Morning, Everyone!

It is Tuesday. It is the <u>first</u> Tuesday of 2005. It is <u>rainy</u> and wet.

We will continue with multiplication during math.

Choose one cell in this multiplication chart and fill in the correct answer.

x	0	1	2	3	4
2	0	2	4	6	8
3	0	3	6	9	12
4	0	4	8	12	16
5	0	5	10	15	20
6	0	6	12	18	24

Once students have worked with full multiplication tables in math, a partial table that can be set up and filled in quickly on the message chart provides an opportunity for review.

Today's greeting:
Eduardo

January 7, 2005

Good Morning, Third Graders!

We will be at a meeting from 9:15 until about 10:00. Ximena is the Guest Teacher Helper this week, but it's everyone's job to be helpful to Ximena and the guest teacher.

It looks like we're going to have some snow today. What do you enjoy about snow?

Your teachers,
Mrs. Meza and Mrs. Fisher

You get to make snow angels N. A.

I enjoy nothing about it TL

Me gusta jugar con bolas de nieve EM

building a snowman S.O.

I like to do snowfights! JS

You can have a sleigh ride TK

I like to play with the snow D.M.

I enjoy throwing snowballs D.M.

Making angels C.P.

You can make a snowman family P.M.

This chart prepares the class to begin the day with a substitute teacher.

Students could also be directed to answer a question such as this by making a quick sketch or using stick figures.

<u>January 11, 2005</u>

Dear Trip Takers,

Today is our trip to the Bruce Museum. If the weather turns snowy, we might not be able to go today. We will certainly go another day.

When we go, how can we act to make our trip go well?

We can't run   You need to behave.

We need to listen

You can't jump on your seat.

Pay attention.

We need to be good.
We need to listen.

These ideas were used to begin a class discussion about field trip behavior. Later, the class might meet again to finish the discussion and create a set of written guidelines to take on their trip.

Dear Writers,

This morning, we will continue to write our playground stories. Remember to have all your details ready before you begin to write.

What is the big problem in your story?

> The ball went over the fence. TK
> My friend fell down S.O.
> My friend fell down D.M.
> I broke a window D.T.
> The big red car squished our kickball because the car ran over our kickball.

The purpose of this message is to engage students in thinking about their stories. Responses like these could spark a rich discussion during morning meeting. You might ask students what they notice about the class's ideas, whether they can think of playground problems that don't involve personal or property damage, or what sorts of details these stories might include.

<u>January 18, 2005</u>

Good Morning, <u>Chilly</u> Children,

It's a really <u>cold</u> day. Even though it is sunny outside, the weather forecast says the <u>temperature</u> is below 10°F.

During writing time we will talk about your hopes and dreams for the rest of the year.

Start thinking and get ready to share:

Do you remember your hopes and dreams from the beginning of the school year? Have you made progress toward reaching them?

At mid-year, this class revisited the goals they had set for themselves in September. They reflected on their progress and decided whether to keep the same goals for the rest of the year or to set new ones. This message got them started on this endeavor.

Good Morning!

Later today, we will listen to "A Gift of Song" and sing along with the CD.

Many families have special ways of giving each other gifts. What is your family's tradition about exchanging gifts?

Hacemos una fiesta bailando, comiendo y abriendo regalos.

We have a party and I give my dad and mom a present and they give me a present. P.M.

We open our presents

We have a party. O.M.

They give presents to me. And I give presents to them. DT

We make a party and we dance. We eat different food. DM

I give presents when it is a birthday. DH

My mom writes the names of all the people coming to the party. You choose a name and you give a present to the person.

By connecting academic and social learning, Rosalea helps students broaden their understanding of the words "gift" and "tradition," while building community knowledge.

<u>January 27, 2005</u>

Good Morning, Chilly Children.

It is another cold day. It was 5°F at my house this morning.

At 2:45 we will have a guest come in to see our Shared Reading lesson on the song "A Gift of Song."

What questions have you had as you read the words to "A Gift of Song"?

? Why did the scarf turn white? S.O.

? ¿Porque ella no podía hablar? E.M.

? Why did Maya want the bird to be blue? L.O

? Why did the blue jay sing? DJ

? Did the blue jay want to turn blue? TK.

? Why did Maya fall in love with the prince? D.M.

? Why did Maya want a voice like the jay bird? DT

?

Collecting and discussing comprehension questions about a class reading gives students the opportunity to learn from each other. It sends the message "We are all learners and together we have powerful community knowledge." Asking this kind of question is also a way for the teacher to check comprehension.

In this class, only a few students had time to write a question before the meeting started. Others would have added their ideas later. To increase participation, consider asking students to write in a notebook or on a sticky note.

The main purpose of this message was to excite students about working with verbs. However, the incorrect use of capital letters in student responses led Rosalea to do a quick review of capitalization during the meeting.

Correcting student responses on the chart is not an everyday practice, but here Rosalea knew students had mastered the rules for capitalization, so spending a small amount of time on misplaced capital letters reminded the class to do their best work on the chart.

February 8, 2005

Good Morning, Third Graders!

Today we'll look at our Word Wall to find verbs.

Write a verb (a word that shows action).

1. hop
2. Jog
3. call
4.
5. Run

6. Dancing
7. Skip (k)
8. Jump Rope (p) (p)
9. Walk
10.

11. Kicking (k)
12.
13.
14.
15.

February 9, 2005

Dear Excellent Readers,

This morning we'll practice reading for details and making inferences as we read.

This afternoon we'll talk about our Native American projects. What projects have you been thinking about? Be ready to talk about your ideas at morning meeting!

As the year goes on, some teachers give students increased responsibility for choosing the greeting for the message. It is still important to make sure that greetings are spelled and punctuated correctly, and that the theme of the greeting (if there is one) fits the theme of the chart.

This class had already begun to learn about "inferences," so including this vocabulary word in the message allowed them to see the word used in context and review its meaning.

Using a "think about" question gave students who didn't have projects in mind time to consider, possibly increasing the number of students who would have ideas to share during morning meeting.

It's typical for children to generate a list of "Don't do's" in response to a question like this. When discussing these responses the teacher might encourage students to rephrase them into a statement about what *to* do. For example, "If we shouldn't press all the buttons at once, what should we do?"

February 14, 2005

Dear Kids,

    We have a new activity for reading at home. Once a week you will take home a tape recorder and listen to a tape of a book. You will read along with the tape.

    How should we take care of our tape recorders? (no repeats)

Keep them up high and not down low.

Don't press all the buttons at once.

I will not let anyone step on it or throw it on the floor.

Don't step on it.

Cuando yo las termine las pondré en su lugar.

To not put it anywhere it could get lost.

<u>February 18, 2005</u>

Dear Third Graders,

   We've been learning about measuring in math. When you need to measure something, how do you decide which tool to use?

   What would you measure with:

a ruler?	a yardstick?	the unit mile?
a book	from the floor to the ceiling	the carpet
a box		the road
a clipboard	a poster	the state
computer	a table	From U.S.A. to Mexico
a t.v.	window	from North America to South America

The activity gives students an immediate try at matching tools with measuring tasks. From their answers, Rosalea could see that some of them needed more work with this skill.

Encouraging children to notice changes in the classroom helps build a sense of community about the space. This list of observations could lead in to a more formal library orientation later in the day.

February 28, 2005

Dear Students,

Welcome back after our long vacation. It looks like we're going to have more snow today.

Mrs. Meza and I have worked very hard to organize the classroom library. What do you notice about how the library has changed?

(no repeats)

I notice that the library is more clean.

I notice that there are big changes.

Yo noto de que hay nuevos libros de música.

I notice that the chapter books are labeled.

That you took the new books from the blue tub and now the chapter books are in the blue tub.

There's a new shelf.

There are more books.

There's a lot of new books.

11:15 recess

March 2, 2005

Good Morning,

Think about how you want to practice your Word Wall words later today. You may practice alone or with a classmate.

What's a Word Wall word you use a lot?

even   about   again   friend

between   because   called

about   complete

clean

friend

This message offers several different jumping off points for discussion during morning meeting, such as sharing different ways to practice, comparing the benefits of practicing with a partner and practicing alone, and using Word Wall words in sentences.

Good Morning, Measurers.

Welcome back after a snowy day. We hope you were able to play in the snow yesterday. How much snow do you think fell yesterday?

Think—What unit of measure would you use to find out?

This message reinforces the class's continuing study of measurement by presenting a concrete situation to which they can apply their understanding.

Framing this as a "think about" question gives each child a chance to consider independently. Then, during meeting, children can compare their answers and the reasoning behind them.

Find Word Wall words in today's message.

March 10, 2005

Dear Children,

(Whether) we go outside for recess depends on the (weather). (We'll) wait and see. (We'll) watch (during) the day.

How are you feeling (about) yesterday's writing prompt?

I felt surprised (because) I didn't know that we were going to have it yesterday,

Excited (because) it's fun to write!

I am feeling happy (because) I liked it when I said, "I don't know how to stop."

I am feeling glad (because) I finished. And (because) I used everything that I learned in writing.

I felt happy (because) I finished.

Rosalea deliberately used Word Wall words in this message. During morning meeting, the class was challenged to see how many Word Wall words they could find.

The class found Word Wall words in their responses, too.

March 22, 2005

Good Morning, Everyone.

It's a <u>sunny</u> / <u>bright</u> day. The sun is shining, and
the temperature is going up. Spring is <u>right</u> / <u>getting</u> / <u>definitely</u>
here! I <u>thought</u> / <u>believed</u> / <u>worried</u> it would never arrive.

What is your favorite season?

Bar Graph

	NA		
	CV		
	DJ		
	JS		
	DG		
	LO		CA
	SO		PM
	DT		DH
	BO		XM
	JB		EM
Spring	Summer	Fall	Winter

Coming up with several words that would make sense for each blank and then reading the paragraph aloud with different combinations can be a fun challenge.

This class answered the same question at the beginning of the year. By comparing that message with this one, the class could see how their opinions had shifted over the winter.

Setting up the response space this way allows for a review of bar graphs.

March 23, 2005

Dear Children,

We will learn one more letter in script this morning. So far we have learned "a" and "c."

How do you feel about learning script so far?

Bar Graph

It's fun!	It's OK	It's hard for me.
NA		
DM		
JB		
AA		
LO		
OM		CA
ED		CF
XM		JS
SO		DT
DH		DH

The results of this poll gave Rosalea insight about students' early experiences learning a new skill and created an opportunity for students to think together about ways to help each other.

Repeating a format like this reinforces learning.

This message supports and encourages children who might be nervous about taking tests. It reminds them that they have prepared, communicates that they will practice again during the day, and expresses their teachers' confidence in them.

April 5, 2005

Dear Math Test-Takers,

The Math 1 test begins at 10:30 a.m. The test will take 60 minutes. That's one hour. We know you are ready.

After Gym we will review the math test-taking strategies you've learned so they will be fresh in your mind right before you take the test. What are some math test-taking strategies you remember?

April 7, 2005

Happy Birthday, Petro.

Let's try to finish writing our poetry words on the sentence strips today. Then we can begin to create our poems.

What will the topic of your poem be?

I have no idea. DM

My family TL

I don't know. SO

My topic is going to be about my family. OM

I don't know?! JS

I don't know. JB

My topic is about my big sister. EM

Students decided on this "Happy Birthday" greeting. Some teachers announce student birthdays in the message; others use an announcement in the corner of the chart.

When asking a question like this, it's a good idea to have a plan for how to help students who don't know their topic yet. One way is to ask students who do have a topic to explain how they made their decisions.

April 8, 2005

Buenos Días, Niños.

After morning meeting, we will welcome our guests from Cheshire, CT. They are here to see and hear your poetry.

Do you like poetry? Why or why not? Answer with a complete sentence.

I like poetry because you can make a poem that rhymes. EM

I like poetry because it rhymes. J.B.

I like poetry because you get to write about the things you like a lot. OM

I like poetry because you can make the words however you want, and it doesn't have to rhyme. CP

Yes, because you can make up your own poems, and I like poems. S.O.

Rosalea asked students to respond using complete sentences because they were practicing that skill. A trade-off is that writing out long answers takes longer, so fewer students have time to write on the chart.

If full participation is a high priority, the teacher could reframe a question like this as a "yes or no" chart and then ask students to explain their answer to a partner during morning meeting.

<u>April 14, 2005</u>

<u>Dear Problem Solvers,</u>

In shared reading today, we'll learn about animals that have invaded the United States, and about the many problems they are causing. What kinds of problems could be caused by animals? Think about this while you answer the question below.

What do you remember about what all animals need to survive?

They need food. They need water.

Animals need air. Animals need to live and they need protection.

They need shelter.

Animals need food and shelter to live. Animals need care.

Exploring challenging words in the message during the meeting can help students learn vocabulary and practice figuring out what words mean from context. This is most effective when only one or two "hard words" are included in a message.

By recalling what they know, students create a common fund of background knowledge to draw on when considering the more challenging question in the first paragraph.

At this point in the year, students will be interested in each other's vacation activities, but it's also important to include content in the message that will help them reengage with schoolwork.

April 25, 2005

Good Morning, Everyone!

Welcome back after a long, sunny, warm vacation. We hope you had a great time.

We will learn 5 new Word Wall words today.

What was your best moment during vacation? Answer using a complete sentence.

I visited an Indian Museum! Mrs. Fisher

My best moment was when I went to the park.

My best moment during vacation was going to Disney World. E.M.

I went on a trip with Stephanie. TL

My best moment was that I found a cat. CP

My best moment was when I went to New York. D.M.

I went on a trip with Tristan. S.O.

My best moment was when I went to Virginia. A.A.

My best moment was when I went to my cousin's house. D.T.

April 27, 2005

Dear Poem Readers,

It's a rainy day. I am thinking about Langston Hughes's poem about rain. His last line was "And I love the rain."

How do you feel about rain?

( ) When it's raining I feel glad because I can do races with my sister.

( ) I feel happy S.O.

(C.F.) I feel glad when it rains because it is nice to hear it.

(O.M.) I feel sad because it is not my favorite season.

(C.H.) You can play outside.

(D.M.) I feel like playing outside today.

(T.K.) I hate it when it rains.

(B.O.) I feel very happy.

( )

(J.B.) I don't like it because we can't go outside to play.

In a case like this, the teacher might read the poem aloud during morning meeting, have the group read it together, or display it so students can read it on their own.

When students' responses are difficult to understand, remember to have them explain what they meant. If possible, find time later to help them revise what they wrote on the chart.

By now the class had mastered most of the alphabet in cursive. Writing parts of the message in cursive at this stage gives students a chance to practice reading cursive, and conveys Rosalea's confidence in the students' newly acquired skill.

Reading in cursive can be challenging for students. Use it sparingly at first, increasing the amount of the message written in cursive as you observe that all students can read it confidently.

April 29, 2005

Good Morning, Poets.

We will take our nature poetry walk. We will take clipboards and observe and draw.

What do you think we'll see on our walk? Let's try and list as many different things as we can.

a tree I think I am going to see lots of birds. We will see birds in the sky.

Lots of trees and little birds. I think we are going to see grass.

We are going to see all natural things?

I think we are going to see birds.

We are going to see leaves.

a bird I think we are going to see trees and plants.

After reading these responses during morning meeting, the class might count the number of "different things" they thought of and add more ideas to the list.

<u>May 11, 2005</u>

<u>Dear</u> <u>Writers,</u>

Today we'll have our last writing prompt for the year. You have learned so much about planning and writing a story! We know you will do well.

What do good writers do when they write?

They think about what they are going to write.

Writers think about the 5 W's—who, what, why, when, where

When they finish they re-read it.

When they finish they edit.

They think about what they know.

They think that they have to read it again.

They write about the things that they are going to write.

The students have been learning and practicing writing strategies all year. Inviting them to name those strategies on the day of a formal writing assessment puts them in a "can-do" frame of mind.

2:05 Mrs. Meza + Mrs. Fisher— meeting

May 20, 2005

Buenos Días,

We will go to the computer lab again this morning at 11:30 a.m. The goal is for everyone to finish entering his or her rough draft today.

What photos have you taken for your project so far?

This information could be used in several ways during morning meeting: If the goal is to get more photos taken, the class could compare their choices of subjects and brainstorm about other things to photograph. Or they could problem-solve about overcoming obstacles.

(E.M.) Tradición: carnaval

(DM) My Aunt's pets.

(TL) my sister

(J.B) My family

(D.O) cloth from my country

(O.M.) I took pictures of my cousin, my cat, and my basketball hoop

(A.A) Un retrato de mi hermano

(L.O) I took a photo of my grandmother and my dad. And my grandma took a photo of my grandpa and me

(DG) My pets

(B.O) I took a picture of forks, knives, and spoons.

(DJ) My aunts and mom

(C.A) Y tomé un retrato de mi familia

Be my editor!

May 23, 2005

Hola,

_aafter music we'll learn two new cursive letters: r and s._wwe'll also work on our photo journals._wwe'll begin with a self-edit.

What are some things editors look for when they edit? (no repeats!)

Bad spelling

look for periods   for punctuation

for commas

            In letters, date

    capital, lower case   They look for
                                mistakes
For question
        marks

As the year progresses, "be my editor" tasks become more challenging. Many teachers save the year's messages to show students how the complexity of later tasks differs from earlier ones. Such a comparison can provide powerful evidence of learning for the children.

June 3, 2005

<u>Good</u> <u>Morning,</u> <u>Children.</u>

This afternoon we will go to the Spring Show at 1:30. What parts are you looking forward to?

We will need to be a respectful audience so everyone will enjoy the show. Think about what we can do to show our respect, and get ready to share your ideas.

A follow-up chart for the day after this one could ask students what they enjoyed about the Spring Show, and what respectful behaviors they noticed.

Mrs. Meza is out.
Guest teacher is
Mr. Rodriguez.

June 9, 2005

Good Morning, Readers.

Today is the last day for small group reading.

What's something that makes you happy about your work in reading this year?

I went up to 38. O.M.
I am a better reader this year. C.V.

I can read level red.

I learned more.

First I was at level 38, and now I am at level 40. DM

I moved up levels.

I feel happy because I have a high level. And there are good books to read!!! DT

Since my first day of school I'm doing better.

I am happy to learn words I don't know.

As the year came to a close, Rosalea used the message to spark student reflections about their accomplishments. Answering questions like this—and reading classmates' answers—can be an effective lead-in to more formal end-of-year self-assessments.

The message sets a reflective, celebratory tone for the final day of school. The student responses could lead in to more in-depth reflection about the year later in the day.

June 17, 2005

Goodbye, Third Graders!

It's the last day of school. We have been together for 181 days! Now it's time to move on.

What would you like to say about our year together?

It was a great year. D.M.

I would like to say that it was a great year.

Some people were nicer this year. SO

It was very fun being together. C.P.

It was a good day and a good year. O.M.

That this was an exciting year. C.V.

It was fun being together. I am going to miss you a lot. L.O.

Messages from a
5th Grade
Classroom

ERIC HENRY

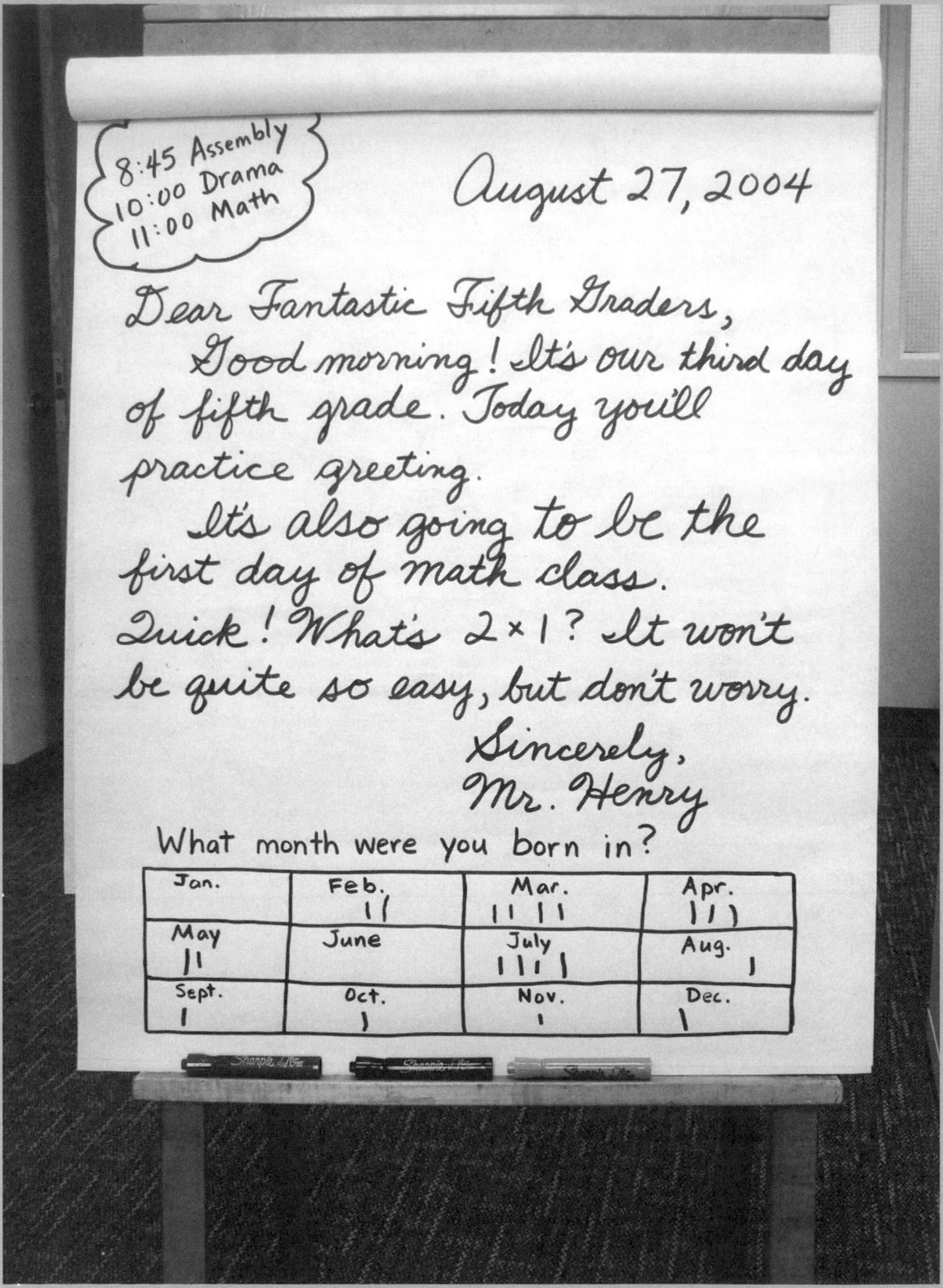

Morning Messages for Fifth Graders

ERIC HENRY

5ᵗʰ grade teacher, John Middleton Elementary School, Skokie, Illinois

THE MORNING MEETING MESSAGE IS AN ANCHOR in my classroom. I could not start a day without one. It's the first place children stop when they enter the room. A transition from the school bus to the classroom, the chart focuses children's attention on the business of school, and it gives them a sense of purpose and belonging in the classroom. It's a place for them to read a friendly message from me, to exchange a word or two with classmates, and to prepare for the day's work.

I try to keep my messages brief and to the point, and to make them interactive in ways that don't require students to do a lot of writing on the chart. Fifth graders at my school usually have fairly strong reading skills and do a lot of work involving reading each day. Therefore, they read the message more to find out what it says than to practice reading. Coming up with content that will engage them is very important. I often write about what the class will be learning that day and use the message as a springboard from morning meeting right into our work.

I also use the chart to give students daily practice in skills we're learning. For example, I sometimes embed mini spelling, grammar, or punctuation lessons by making deliberate errors on the chart and having students find and correct them. Or I purposely use con-

tent area vocabulary—words like "patriot," "loyalist," "prime numbers," and "tributaries." Other times the chart challenges the children to think creatively about something, and always, it gives them practice in following directions.

I also use the chart to motivate the group. The message often lets them know how well they're doing in certain areas. If I'm going to be absent, I always write a chart to the class to remind them to do their best work while I'm away for the day.

School and Classroom Demographics

John Middleton Elementary School is in Skokie, a suburb of Chicago that's known for its good schools, safe neighborhoods, and strong sense of community. The school, a grade 1–5 school with about 600 students, is extremely diverse ethnically. The children's backgrounds include African, Puerto Rican, Pakistani, Romanian, Indian, Assyrian, Filipino, Ukrainian, Bulgarian, Cuban, Colombian, and other heritages. There are children of Jewish, Muslim, Christian, and other faiths, as well as those whose families do not practice or lean toward any religion. Families' incomes range from lower middle to upper middle. Most students come from two-parent homes.

During the year from which the following messages were taken, our class had fourteen boys and nine girls, ages ten and eleven. Two of these students spent most of their day in a developmentally appropriate special needs classroom but were always included in morning meeting, field trips, and social activities such as parties.

The Children's Academic and Social Abilities

Academically, this class reflected the bell curve one sees in many classrooms. The students' reading ability ranged from about third through sixth grade at the beginning of the year. By year's end most children were reading in the fourth through seventh grade range. Four students received all their reading, spelling, and writing instruction in a pull-out ESL class, while another three received ESL support in writing only. Although this was a class of good writers and spellers overall, most students would read independently for pleasure only after much coaxing and prodding. There were a few avid readers, however, and some who grew to enjoy reading as the year progressed. One student whose greatest interest was hockey began the year not liking reading at all. But by the end of the year, he was completely hooked on the *Series of Unfortunate Events* books.

Math and social studies were favorite subjects. The students made excellent progress overall in math, with average class grades always in the mid to upper eighties on quizzes, tests, and projects.

In the social realm, there was a general climate of openness and friendliness in the classroom. We owed this in part to our community-building classroom routines and practices —morning meeting in particular. At the beginning of the year students' prior experience with morning meeting varied, and I taught the routine step by step. This was time well spent. Morning meeting gave the students, including the students with special needs, a safe structure to practice being part of a cohesive group. This class looked forward to it. For instance, on field trip days, we'd often only have time for a quick greeting before we got on the bus. When we returned to school they'd almost always ask, "Can we do the rest of morning meeting now?"

That said, cultivating a community where everyone felt safe and included was an ongoing learning process for this class, which had some pretty strong personalities. As children their age do, they sometimes argued, teased, and called each other names. When problems arose, the social skills we had practiced helped us get through them. I was impressed overall by how willing these students were to accept differences and by the sincerity of their apologies.

The high ratio of boys to girls in the class brought some challenges as well. I worked hard to keep the boys from dominating discussions, and making groups that encouraged the quiet girls to assert themselves was tricky. By the end of the year I had changed the seating arrangement a dozen times!

My Teaching Approach

I have been teaching for fourteen years. I began by teaching fourth grade in an inner city Chicago school, then transferred to a different inner city school, where I taught fourth and fifth grades. For the last nine years I've been teaching fifth grade at Middleton in Skokie.

Two of my deepest convictions about teaching are that children need to learn first and foremost how to get along peacefully in a democratic society, and that children learn best through social interaction. My aim, therefore, is to create a classroom where everyone has a voice and where many activities are done in partnerships or small groups. I teach them to use cooperative learning strategies, and I strive to model respect and integrity, whether it's taking care of people or things. I don't spend much time talking in front of the class, but encourage the children instead to take responsibility for their own learning as much as possible. During fifth grade, students regularly do research, write reports, and present their learning to one another.

My classroom tends to be orderly, both in its physical setup and in the way I conduct activities and lessons. Physically, the room is neat, with a minimum of clutter. Lessons, meanwhile, have a beginning, middle, and end. A typical lesson begins with a warm-up followed by instruction, student practice of some sort, and a closing review. We spend some time every day reviewing the previous day's learning, and I also spend a good deal of time teaching students how to learn. We work on study skills, for example, and practice doing homework at school before the real homework starts going home.

Fifth graders at my school are the oldest children in the building, and the amount of work they are expected to do is genuinely challenging. It's important for me to let them know that I see how grown-up they are, but also that even though they are not little kids anymore, we can still have fun learning together. In my classroom, morning meeting and the message chart are essential to building a community where learning is challenging but fun, and where through hard work, responsibility, and cooperation we can all achieve our goals.

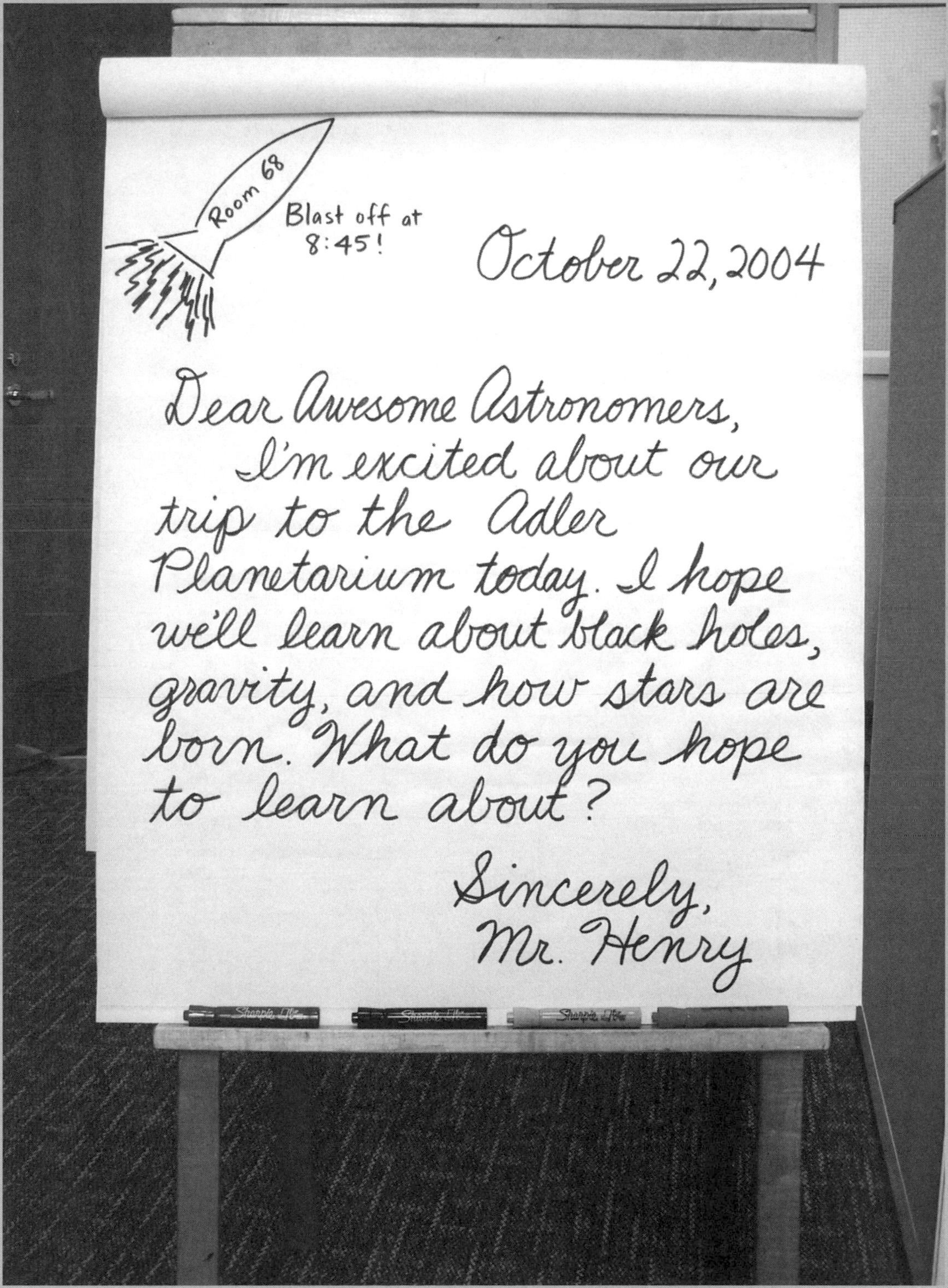

August 27, 2004

Dear Fantastic Fifth Graders,

Good morning! It's our third day of fifth grade. Today you'll practice greeting.

It's also going to be the first day of math class. Quick! What's 2 x 1? It won't be quite so easy, but don't worry.

Sincerely,
Mr. Henry

Jan.	Feb.	Mar.	Apr.
	||	||||	||\
May	June	July	Aug.
||		||\\\|	|
Sept.	Oct.	Nov.	Dec.
|	|	|	|

Eric teaches the students a variety of ways to greet each other during morning meeting. Learning and practicing greetings together—even for students familiar with morning meeting and greeting—helps the class build community at the beginning of the year.

Birthdays are a topic that students naturally find interesting, but collecting this information about birth months has value for the teacher, too. It helps Eric understand the students' developmental needs throughout the year.

8:45 Assembly
10:00 Drama
11:00 Math

August 31, 2004

Dear Friendly Fifth Graders,

Since today is an early dismissal day, we'll have a quick greeting. What is one way you can make even a quick greeting feel friendly?

Sincerely,
Mr. Henry

In your journal, write about the way you want our class to be.

Example: I want our class to be a friendly place where everyone learns as much as possible.

By putting schedule changes and other "housekeeping" announcements in a corner rather than in the message, you can alert students that the information is important, while keeping the message focused on the topic you've selected.

Messages written in cursive give students at this level needed practice in reading script. To ensure that all students can read messages in cursive, wait until they have begun using it for their own written work.

This message communicates that friendliness is valued in this classroom. By asking students to think about behaviors that make greetings feel friendly, Eric encourages them to see friendliness as a skill they can learn and practice.

This class begins the process of creating classroom rules by deciding on individual "Hopes and Dreams"—their goals for the year. The rules they agree upon will be designed to make the classroom a place where each person can achieve his or her hopes and dreams.

September 2, 2004

Dear Learners,

Good morning! Today we will finish Hopes and Dreams. Be ready to share one important thing you want to learn about, practice, or get better at in 5th grade.

Sincerely,
Mr. Henry

Whether they are familiar with morning messages or not, at the beginning of the year, students need to be taught how to use the chart, including when to read it, how and when to write on it, and what is expected when the message says to think or "be ready to share" about a topic.

Happy Birthday, Tooba!

September 8, 2004

Dear Students,

Buenos días. That means "good morning" in Spanish. Can you think of some places where people greet each other in the morning by saying "buenos días"?

We will have our first computer lesson at 9:20. I'll teach you a few things about using Microsoft Word.

Sincerely,
Mr. Henry

Does your family
have email at home?

Yes	No	Don't Know
~~||||~~ ~~||||~~ ~~||||~~ |||	||	

Questions in the body of the message can encourage thinking and engagement. At the beginning of the year, Eric shows students how to tell whether to write their answers on the chart or come to morning meeting with an answer in mind.

During the meeting, students may talk about what they already know about Microsoft Word. That information might lead Eric to adjust his lesson plans. Similarly, the question about email access helps Eric assess his options for communicating with families.

Music & Art

September 17, 2004

Dear Students,

Bonjour! That's "good morning" in french. What are some countries where most people speak french? Today we will continue our geography study.

Sincerely,
Mr. Henry

Eric makes deliberate errors on the chart and asks students to identify and correct them during morning meeting.

During meeting, Eric would ask students to share ideas about countries where French is spoken, and would be prepared to supply a few answers himself if necessary. They might locate the countries they named on a map or globe.

Write a geography word that you know.

globe   sea

Mountain Range   Equator

longitude   latitude   bay   Delta   tributary

gulf   Peninsula

Prime Meridian

Delta

9-23-04

Dear Class,

I'll miss you today while you take good care of Mrs. Pokorny. Give her your signed rules paper and do your best. I'll see you Friday!

Sincerely,
Mr. Henry

In the upper elementary grades, teachers often vary the way they write the date. The first time Eric uses an abbreviated form like this one, during morning meeting he would check to make sure all students know what each number represents.

By leaving this message to greet students as they arrive, Eric establishes a positive tone and communicates his expectations for student behavior on a day when they will have a substitute teacher.

After working deliberately with the class to create a safe class environment for several weeks, Eric checks in about how the classroom rules are working. Setting this up as a "quick share" so that each person has a chance to respond briefly communicates that everyone's answers are welcomed and valued.

9-29-04

Dear Rule Makers,

Good morning! How do you think our rules are working? Be ready to do a quick share about this question at morning meeting.

Sincerely,
Mr. Henry

Daniel Cryzlyn
Thursday Shares (2)

Responsive Classroom morning meetings include a sharing component. After several weeks of practicing this component, Eric invites students to sign up for sharing on a future date. This class later transitioned to using a weekly schedule posted elsewhere that allowed them to plan further ahead.

October 1, 2004

Dear Class,

BOO! Yes, it's that month of ghosts and goblins, October. I'm not really a big fan of Halloween, but I really enjoy the weather in autumn. What's one thing you like about this season?

Sincerely,
Mr. Henry

David Fiona
2 Shares for Monday

Eric deliberately leaves out the apostrophes so that the students, who have been learning to use this punctuation mark, can practice by finding and correcting the errors. The class decides where the apostrophes should be added during morning meeting, and students write them on the chart.

Eric occasionally writes messages focused on sharing personal opinions or experiences. When the group shares responses during meeting, they learn about each other and practice listening and discussion skills.

Eric's tone keeps this message about a new seating arrangement positive and friendly. During meeting, after sharing what they notice, students might talk about the benefits that rearranging the seating every so often could have for everyone.

October 4, 2004

Dear Class,

Good morning! We have a new seating arrangement that I think will work well for everyone. What do you notice about it?

Sincerely,
Mr. Henry

Tooba, Benjamin
Wednesday Shares

October 8, 2004

Dear Cooperative Class,

Good morning! I'm feeling much better today. Mr. Duncan wrote that he enjoyed your enthusiasm. How do you feel about how the day went yesterday?

Your teacher,
Mr. Henry

Using the message to give positive feedback can be a powerful method of reinforcement. Here, Eric creates an opportunity for the class to discuss what Mr. Duncan might have meant by "enthusiasm" and to take responsibility for assessing their own behavior as well.

Like many teachers at this level, Eric varied the way the message was read during meeting, alternating among choral reading, selecting individuals to read, and reading it aloud himself. He also sometimes asked students to read silently and then had someone summarize in his or her own words.

October 12, 2004

Dear Awesome Astronomers,

I hope you enjoyed the autumn weather over the long weekend.

Today is the first day of Starlab, a portable planetarium. Have you ever been to a planetarium? What do you think Starlab will be like? We'll begin star searching at 10:30.

Sincerely,
Mr. Henry

This message builds interest in a new topic of study and incorporates topical vocabulary words such as "astronomers" and "planetarium." During morning meeting, the class might talk about what a planetarium is and what a "portable" one might be like.

Students' positive responses to this question led Eric to use "hobbies" as a theme for the sharing portion of morning meetings in upcoming weeks.

Do you have a hobby?

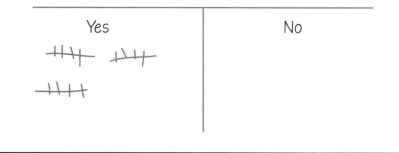

Yes	No
̶H̶H̶ ̶H̶H̶ ̶H̶H̶	

October 13, 2004

Dear Class,

Since we have had our class meeting about it, the Thinking Chair is now available for everyone. How do you think having a Thinking Chair will affect our classroom?

Sincerely,
Mr. Henry

Should our class choose a different name for the Thinking Chair?

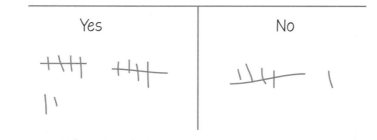

Yes	No
✝✝✝ ✝✝✝ ‖	‖✝✝ ‖

Like many *Responsive Classroom* teachers, Eric uses a positive time-out area in the classroom, here called the "Thinking Chair," as a non-punitive way for students to collect themselves when they begin to lose self-control. This question allows him to check their understanding of the purpose of this procedure.

Now that the group has practiced the time-out procedure, Eric responds to negative feelings some students expressed about the name by putting it to a vote.

In this message, Eric sparks students' curiosity about what a "reading road trip" will be and lets them know how they might find answers to some of their questions before meeting.

During meeting, the class might talk about what a person would do and say when sharing about a hobby and how an audience could listen and respond respectfully. Once expectations were clear, students could start signing up, as this class did on October 20th.

October 18, 2004

Dear Readers,

Today we're going on a "reading road trip." See the poster on the blue bulletin board for more details.

Sincerely,
Mr. Henry

Think about your hobby.

What's one interesting thing you could tell your classmates about it?

October 20, 2004

Dear Students,

We'll be writing a class report today on the coral reef crisis. We'll gather ideas together before we start writing, so think about what you've learned already about coral reefs and the problems on them.

Sincerely,
Mr. Henry

Do you think the problems on coral reefs have ...

Improved	Stayed the same	Gotten worse
	|	ℍℍ ℍℍ

Benjamin Oksana
2 Hobby Shares for tomorrow

With this chart Eric helps students warm up for the writing activity they'll complete later in the day. During meeting, the class might hear from a couple of volunteers who would explain their responses to the question at the end of the chart. This could help everyone think through his or her position more carefully.

On the day of a field trip, Eric uses the message to model enthusiasm and active thinking before a field trip. The class would share their ideas about what they hoped to learn before departure.

Room 68

Blast off at
8:45!

October 22, 2004

Dear Awesome Astronomers,

I'm excited about our trip to the Adler Planetarium today. I hope we'll learn about black holes, gravity, and how stars are born. What do you hope to learn about?

Sincerely,
Mr. Henry

Check the job board!

October 25, 2004

Dear Class,

Another new room design! Please notice the new seating arrangement. I think it will work well for everyone.

During meeting we'll talk briefly about these changes.

Sincerely,
Mr. Henry

Even though he may feel frustrated about having to rearrange the seating again, Eric resists using the message to scold the class. By using a positive, matter-of-fact tone, he helps students start the day in a productive frame of mind for addressing a classroom problem.

Discussion about this message might include talking about what a "responsible citizen" is and how voting relates to that concept, students' theories about why few people voted in recent elections, and why they think more will vote that day. This topic could be continued after the election.

11/2/04

Dear Great Group,

Today is Election Day. I think voting is an important part of being a responsible citizen. Unfortunately, in recent elections only about 50% of people voted. Why do you think this is?

Sincerely,
Mr. Henry

What percentage of Americans do you think will vote today?

50%   75%   65% 90% 85%
    70%   85%   70%   75%
        99%   50%   60%
    66%   60%
        85%

Nov. 10, 2004

Dear Gregarious Group,

Good morning! Are you feeling gregarious today? I hope so. Today the whole 5th grade will gather in the cafeteria to work on a storytelling project together. I hope you have a great day!

Sincerely,
Mr. Henry

Challenging vocabulary words such as "gregarious" can be fun for a class to figure out as a group. This message provides some context, so the class can try to guess the meaning of the word before finding it in a dictionary.

Nov. 12, 2004

Dear Hardworking Class,

I hope you got to relax on Veterans Day.

Do you know anyone who is a veteran?

yes	no	don't know
~~HHH~~ ~~HHH~~ I	I I \	I I I \

It's not necessary to sign the message every day, especially if doing so interferes with the flow of content.

The "don't know" responses tell Eric that the class may need a quick review of what "veteran" means.

Quick Share for tomorrow: What book are you reading right now? If you don't have a book now, choose one before tomorrow!

11/18/04

Dear Cooperative Class,

Good morning! I was impressed by your focus and spirited play during yesterday's Explorer Matrix game. Wow! What are some things that you think made this activity go so well for us?

Sincerely,
Mr. Henry

Write a word or phrase about exploration.

route   to find riches

New World   Pilgrims

Francisco Coronado   John Cabot

Motives   Henry Hudson

Robert de la Salle   Christopher Columbus

Jacques Cartier

Friday: Quick Share - one fact about the Age of Exploration

By naming specific positive behaviors that he noticed, Eric provides students with examples of what he thinks made the activity go well. This may help them come up with ideas of their own to share during meeting.

December 1, 2004

Dear Fifth Graders,

Today is the first day of the last month of the year!

Two people in our class share a birthday on December 30th. Do you know who they are?

Hint: Both are musicians.

Sincerely,
Mr. Henry

Students at this grade level often enjoy puzzles. Occasional messages focused on class riddles can be a fun way to encourage students to learn about each other.

Announcements:
Seating Arrangement,
Readiness

12/2/04

Dear Class,

Good morning! Today you'll learn a method of note taking for research writing. Then you will begin researching your explorer. What are some things you hope to find out about your explorer?

Your teacher,
Mr. Henry

Eric uses a corner bubble to alert the class about several announcements he wants to make, but keeps the message focused on an engaging academic topic. This reinforces that while seating arrangements and readiness are important issues, the focus of the day will be on research and learning about explorers.

By using words with the patterns the class has been studying, Eric shows that their spelling words can be used to communicate in a real piece of writing. The task provides a quick, confidence building warm-up for students on the day of a test.

12/3/04

Dear Super Spellers,

Good morning! I hope I will marvel at your final spelling of our list of words with more than one syllable. If you earn a 100% on the test, please be humble and don't brag about it.

Sincerely,
Mr. Henry

Write any word with an /ᵊl/ ending in the correct row.

el – angel Marvel

al – original festival Principal general

il – council pupil fossil evil

le – apple angle Scramble little People

December 6, 2004

Dear Astronomers,

Good morning! Did you notice all the new astronomy books in our classroom library? This week we'll be learning about stars, galaxies, and solar systems. What do you already know about them from working with Starlab and visiting the planetarium?

Sincerely,
Mr. Henry

Prepare for a short writing assessment by putting a heading on writing paper.

This message builds student interest in continuing to learn about astronomy. It mentions new topics and library resources for students to look forward to, and reminds them that they already have background knowledge about the general topic of astronomy.

On very busy days, Eric sometimes uses a bubble at the bottom of the chart to give directions so that students can get right to work at the end of morning meeting. This gives students practice following written directions and makes the transition more efficient.

Messages that give honest, supportive feedback can serve as a mirror for students and help them take pride in their accomplishments. They can also provide students with the encouragement they need to keep working hard.

12-10-04

Dear Hardworking Fifth Graders,

I know how tough it can be to concentrate when winter break is coming up, and I noticed how much effort and focus you've put in this week. Let's all keep doing our best today.

Sincerely,
Mr. Henry

notice new jobs today

December 13, 2004

Dear Explorer Experts,

This morning feels like winter – only 26°F. This final week of school before vacation will be fun and busy. Today we'll hear the first explorer reports.

Sincerely,
Mr. Henry

This message acknowledges that the upcoming winter vacation is on students' minds and reminds them that they still have a lot to accomplish before then. By concluding with a statement about what will happen today, Eric helps students begin the day focused on classroom work.

This message helps students reconnect to school after a vacation. Simple tasks such as looking for changes in the classroom and naming something they're looking forward to can help students feel engaged as they begin a new year.

January 3, 2005

Happy New Year, 5th Graders!

I'm excited about the new year ahead of us and all the learning we'll be doing in the coming months. Are you?

Look around the room for things that are new or different.

Sincerely,
Mr. Henry

Write in your journal:

What's one thing you look forward to doing in 2005?

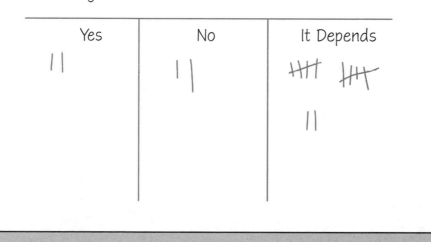

1-5-05

Dear Students,

Today we'll learn about Jamestown, the first permanent English colony in America. What are some reasons people from England might have decided to leave their homes and start a new life in a colony?

Would you have done it?

Yes	No	It Depends
‖	‖|	⊩⊩ ⊩⊩ ‖

The class had already learned about colonies, so they had enough context to think about what a "permanent" colony might be. They might discuss this distinction and review reasons why people became colonists during meeting, or save their thoughts until social studies time later in the day.

The number of "it depends" answers indicates that students appreciate the complexities of the colonists' situations. A rich discussion could begin by having students explain the thinking behind their responses.

Connecting students' experiences to curriculum can stimulate interest in academic topics. On a snowy day, thinking about how colonists would have dealt with winter weather provides a tangible way in to learning about the daily lives of the residents of Jamestown.

1-6-05

Dear Snowy Students,

Good morning! Can you imagine what a hardship snow like this would have been back in 1607 when Jamestown was settled? What are some of the things that would have been hard about dealing with winter weather back then?

Sincerely,
Mr. Henry

1-14-05

Dear Minstrels and Mimes,

Your performance last night at the Madrigal Dinner was amazing! It really seemed as if we were inside a medieval castle.

Today Mrs. Pokorny will be your teacher. Have a great day and a fun long weekend.

Sincerely,
Mr. Henry

Quick Share during Morning Meeting:

Your name and one fact about Jamestown, Roanoke, or Plymouth.

Messages that give genuinely positive feedback can be reinforcing for students, especially if they include specific details that help students understand what they did well.

A quick share on a topic students feel confident about can help set a positive tone at the beginning of a day with a substitute teacher. Eric asks students to say their names as a courtesy to the substitute teacher and to reinforce the presentation skills they have been practicing.

As the class learns about similes, Eric incorporates them in messages. Seeing similes in context shows students how they can be used to enliven writing.

The class works together during the meeting to figure out the mystery word. Students who followed the directions about previewing the packet found clues that helped them solve the puzzle.

1-20-05

Dear Fantastic Food Chemists,

Yesterday's lab tests went as smoothly as a skate on ice. Today we'll learn how to test for a nutrient called

g l u c o s e.

Preview the packet on your desk.

Your teacher,
Mr. Henry

January 21, 2005

Dear Fifth Graders,

Good morning! We are having a special guest from an organization called Junior Achievement. This group teaches children about business and earning a living.

Sincerely,
Mr. Henry

Do you think you'll want to have your own business when you grow up?

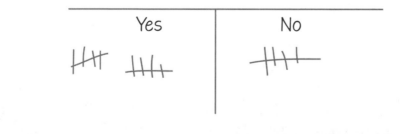

Yes	No
HH HH	HH

This task helps students become engaged with the topic of the presentation before it begins. Making personal connections can be an effective way to build interest in new topics.

Yes/no questions can work well when time before meeting is tight, because students can respond quickly. Students can then elaborate on their responses during meeting. In this case students could describe the kinds of businesses they'd like to have, or explain what about having a business appeals to them (or doesn't).

Following up general affirmations like "you've really learned a lot" by asking the class to name specific skills they've learned provides students with tangible evidence of their accomplishments. Asking students to think about the usefulness of the skills they've learned helps them see that they've been learning for a reason.

2-7-05

Dear Skillful Technology Users,

Mrs. Herbach has a great new computer skill to teach you today. You've really learned a lot in the Computer Lab this year! Which of the skills you've learned has been most useful? Bring your ideas about this to morning meeting.

Sincerely,
Mr. Henry

2-9-05

Dear Careful Chemists,

Today we will be testing liquids for a nutrient called protein. Which liquids do you think we will test? Which do you think will test positive for protein? Write your answers to these questions in your journal.

Sincerely,
Mr. Henry

This chart works as both a warm-up and a confidence booster. Now that they have been studying food chemistry for a while, students have enough experience to make good guesses about what liquids they will be testing and enough background knowledge to make reasonable predictions. Their science work for the day might begin with a discussion of their predictions.

Students at this age care a great deal about what their peers think, but they also still thrive on adult recognition. Publicly displaying their work reinforces students' sense of themselves as community members with important knowledge to share.

2-10-05

Dear Hardworking Class,

Good morning! Your billboard projects are awesome! The information is clear and complete, and the designs are striking. I put them up in the hallway so others can see them and learn from you.

Your teacher,
Mr. Henry

2-15-05

Dear Math Mavens,

Today we will learn about these symbols: in², m², ft², cm². Have you seen them before? Where?

Sincerely,
Mr. Henry

True or false? These shapes have the same area:

Although the abbreviations in², m², ft², and cm² may be unfamiliar to these students, the concept of calculating area as a number of squares is not. The task at the bottom of the chart reminds students of what they already know and serves as a bridge into the new lesson.

When the message is read during meeting, students will learn how the abbreviations are pronounced. This will help them figure out what the symbols mean.

This message reminds students that the recent holiday was Presidents' Day and gives them a few things to puzzle over, including naming the first president of the United States and solving a word problem. Such a message could simply be a fun way to start the day, or it could be used as a springboard to further investigations on the topic of U.S. presidents.

2-22-05

Dear Potential Presidents,

Good morning! Did you enjoy the lengthy weekend? Here's a puzzle for you:

On February 22, 1732, the man who would become our first president was born. How old was he when he took office in 1789?

Sincerely,
Mr. Henry

2/25/05

Dear Class,

Mrs. Pokorny will be your teacher today. Remember our class-room rules.

Sincerely,
Mr. Henry

February 25, 1870

Hiram R. Revels became the first African American

S E N A T O R

Eric uses the message to remind students of their responsibilities as community members at the beginning of a day with a substitute teacher.

The class would work together to solve the mystery word puzzle during morning meeting. This sets a cooperative tone for the day. This puzzle could lead into learning about what senators do, how Hiram Revels was elected, and reasons why there were no African American senators before him.

March 1, 2005

Dear Students,

Today we'll learn about a hero named Casimir Pulaski. What are some ways a person can be a hero? Bring your ideas about heroes to morning meeting.

Sincerely,
Mr. Henry

Do you have a personal hero?

The questions in this message could be a springboard for further investigation, depending on the agenda for the day. Students might respond in journals, compile a list of ideas about heroes, or name and describe their personal heroes. Any of these activities could lead in to learning about Casimir Pulaski.

3/10/05

Dear Intrepid Test Takers,

It's our second day of ISAT, and I think we're doing well. Since many of you finished early yesterday, you can slow down a bit on this morning's tests. Our schedule will be just like yesterday's.

Sincerely,
Mr. Henry

Sharpen your pencil ... and your mind! :)

Eric uses the message to give the class encouragement and advice in the midst of standardized testing. A calm, supportive message can be reassuring for students during a stressful time.

Messages don't have to be complex. This simple, straightforward message gives students something specific to look forward to and creates an opportunity for them to establish expectations for good audience behavior.

March 18, 2005

Dear Class,

Get ready for a day of learning from your friends. We'll hear classroom reports throughout the day. What are some things you can do to stay focused, listen carefully, and be a supportive audience member? We'll share ideas about this at morning meeting.

Sincerely,
Mr. Henry

March 21, 2005

Dear Autobiographical Authors,

Good morning! This week we are having a Writing Workshop. By the end of the week you will have written a story about your life to share with the class.

Your teacher,
Mr. Henry

Take out your Writing Workshop folder.

The idea of writing and sharing their "life story" can be exciting to students at this age. The salutation reinforces the importance of this work by addressing the students as "authors" and offers an opportunity to review what "autobiographical" means.

The context clues allow students to understand the message without needing to know what a character sketch is. During meeting they'll all become familiar with this new term.

Students have learned about adjectives as parts of speech. This task helps them see that adjectives also play a role in their own writing, and gets them started on putting their ideas into words.

March 22, 2005

Dear Writers,

Today you'll write a character sketch of a person you know very well, such as a cousin, an uncle, or a parent. Think about the person you will write about and be prepared to share ideas during morning meeting.

Write an adjective describing the person you will write about.

trustworthy awesome   nice   kind
good all around   sweet   funny
friendly   funny   loving   cool

4-8-05

Dear Hardworking Historians,

We're just about finished with
our unit about the causes of the War
for Independence. We've learned that
there were many reasons why the
war began. Which reason do you
think was the most important?

Proclamation of 1763	Stamp Act |||	Quartering Act ||
Boston Massacre ||	Boston Tea Party	Intolerable Acts |||||	

During the meeting, Eric might simply ask the class to comment on what they noticed about their votes. Later he could refer back to the chart and build upon these answers—for instance, by having individuals explain their reasoning or groups work together to rank the causes from most to least important.

When Eric uses embedded skill review, he waits until meeting to circle the correct response. That gives each student time to think and involves the whole group in deciding on the answer.

If students didn't notice it on their own, Eric would draw their attention to the "blooming" metaphor by, for example, asking about the meaning of the sentence and the images it might create in readers' minds.

4-12-05

Dear Class,

Good morning! Have you noticed the trees in the courtyard? (There / They're) blooming. Today we will see how your writing skills are blooming with some fun activities.

Sincerely,
Mr. Henry

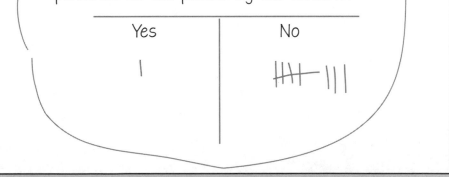

Do you know the name of the writer pictured on the poster by the window?

Yes	No
I	卌 |||

This question is an engaging way to get students to notice something new in the room and gives them something to talk about before morning meeting starts.

April 13, 2005

Dear Writers,

    Today all fifth graders will show their writing skills on a special test. To do well, plan your writing, organize your thoughts, and then do ((your)/you're) best.

Sincerely,
Mr. Henry

Think: What's a topic you've enjoyed writing about this year?

This calm message encourages students on the day of a test by expressing confidence in them and reminding them of writing skills they have learned. The "your/you're" skill practice tacitly reminds students to also remember to pay attention to spelling and mechanics.

This thinking question could help students get into a positive frame of mind about writing before they start the test.

April 18, 2005

Dear Students,

Good morning! A person who is crazy about cars celebrated a birthday on Sunday. Do you know who?

Your teacher,
Mr. Henry

Write a few words about what you did over the weekend.

carwash

played outside

computer

football

sleepover party

Played outside

ate dinner with my family in restaurant

soccer

Played outside a lot and slept

friend's party!

played baseball with my new glove

Sharing about weekend activities can help students start the week feeling connected to their classmates. Getting to know each other is still important at the end of the year. With a question such as this, the group might talk about what they noticed about their responses (e.g., that many of them did things outside).

April 19, 1775

Dear Sons and Daughters of Liberty,

I have some sad and amazing news to report. At about 5:00 this morning, British troops marched into Lexington, Massachusetts and were met on the town's common green by 77 armed colonists. Shots rang out. This means only one thing: war.

Solemnly,
Mr. Henry

Where do you stand?

Patriot	Loyalist
~~IIII~~ III	~~IIII~~ II

Neutralist
I

The class has been learning about early American history, and a playful message encourages students to imagine that they have traveled back in time.

The "Neutralist" choice is offered as an option but located to the side because the class has learned that in this conflict few people were able to remain neutral.

This message helps students get in gear for a field trip by engaging their thinking on various levels. While students' interest will probably be piqued by thinking and talking about the idea of "experiencing" art, balancing this abstract topic with a more concrete task about naming painters ensures that all students will embark on the trip feeling that they know some things about art.

This message is a prime example of the adult-like language Eric uses with the class. Students this age appreciate such recognition of their growing maturity.

April 21, 2005

Dear Art Appreciators,

Today we're visiting a museum that some people think is one of the finest art museums in the country. Your task at the Art Institute will be to experience some art and see if it has any meaning for you.

Sincerely,
Mr. Henry

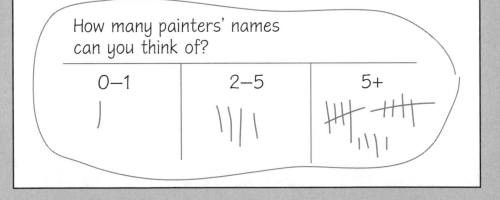

How many painters' names can you think of?

0–1	2–5	5+
I	|||| I	✝✝✝✝ ✝✝✝✝ |||| I

April 25, 2005

Dear Soon-To-Be Sixth Graders,

Today you'll empty out your desk and start keeping everything you need for school in your locker. This is practice for next year. At the middle school you won't have a desk to store things in.

What do you think will be challenging about using a locker instead of a desk?

Sincerely,
Mr. Henry

During their last six weeks of school, the class begins to discuss and prepare for their transition to middle school. Having a locker and traveling from class to class will be a major change for these students. Practicing in a structured, supportive environment helps them develop the skills they need to make this shift successfully.

Before the class visits the local middle school, Eric gathers information about their questions and concerns. Those students who aren't comfortable sharing with the group on this topic can participate by writing their thoughts for Eric to read later.

Take home a permission slip.

May 9, 2005

Dear Students,

Next week we'll go to McCracken Middle School and take a tour. What do you think we'll see? What would you like the tour to include?

You'll have a chance to ask questions while you're there. What questions would you like to ask?

Your teacher,
Mr. Henry

Write your ideas about the questions in the message on a piece of scrap paper before morning meeting.

May 11, 2005

Dear Class,

Wow! Your skits about the
Declaration of independence really
showed how well you have learned
the material. Good luck on the test.

Sincerely,
Mr. Henry

Vote!

Ice Cream	Donuts
ⅠⅠⅠⅠ ⅠⅠⅠⅠ	ⅠⅠⅠⅠ ⅠⅠⅠⅠ
ⅠⅠⅠⅠ ⅠⅠⅠⅠ	ⅠⅠⅠⅠ ⅠⅠ
Ⅰ	

A specific, positive comment sets an encouraging tone on the day of a test. By saying that the class has demonstrated their knowledge of the material, Eric gives them a reason to feel confident.

The class voted for a treat they won as a result of a school contest.

This group has learned a lot about making presentations during the year. Eric celebrates this by using the greeting, "Practiced Presenters," as well as by giving students responsibility for selecting a presentation time.

He doesn't let them get away with the "voting fraud" of the previous day. Without making a big deal out of it, he simply reminds them of the rule for voting and repeats the task on this chart.

May 12, 2005

Dear Practiced Presenters,

Good morning! Today most of you will present your nutrient posters to the class. I put a sign-up sheet on the closet door. Please sign up for a presentation time before morning meeting.

Sincerely,
Mr. Henry

One person, one vote!

Ice Cream	Donuts
||||| ||||| ||||	|||||	

May 16, 2005

Dear Fifth Graders,

You'll probably see dozens of kindergartners in the building this week ~~weak~~. Do you remember being in kindergarten? I cannot.

Sincerely,
Mr. Henry

Think about this:

What are some of your best and worst memories of 5th grade?

Of Middleton Elementary?

This message helps students reflect on how much they have grown and accomplished during their elementary school years. Eric uses humor to lighten the mood a little in this message. Students this age can be fascinated by glimpses of their teachers as real people.

5-18-05

Dear Class,

Today we'll visit your new school. I know that you are all excited about this big step in your lives. Learn as much as you can on the trip, and we'll talk about it when we return.

Sincerely,
Mr. Henry

Think about this:

In which subject do you think you made the best progress this year?

Thinking about their accomplishments helps students embark on the trip to the middle school feeling confident. This question could also be used as a starting point for more extensive year-end self-assessment work.

Throughout the last weeks of school, Eric uses morning messages to encourage reflection and bring closure to the school year. Beginning this process early and maintaining a consistent focus on it conveys its importance to students.

May 20, 2005

Dear Class,

Good morning! On May 20, 1927, Charles Lindbergh left New York on the first solo airplane flight across the Atlantic Ocean. Do you know how many miles that is? How long do you think the flight took?

24 1/2 hours	33 1/2 hours	41 1/2 hours
‖‖‖	‖‖‖ ‖‖‖ ‖‖‖	‖‖‖

An "on this day in history" message about an interesting topic gives students a break from thinking about the end of the year so intensively. The questions Eric asks are appropriately challenging for students at this level; he could provide the answers or challenge students to find them.

The poetic language in this message might lead to a discussion about symbols for endings and beginnings. The message also validates feelings of sadness students may be having about ending the year and leaving elementary school, while acknowledging feelings of excitement and relief that summer is coming.

5-24-05

Dear Fantastic Fifth Graders,

I'm down to my last few pages of chart paper, and my markers are fading. It's a good thing that summer is almost here. In the meantime, let's work our hardest and end the year on a high note.

Sincerely,
Mr. Henry

Write in your journal:

What's one thing you'll miss about Middleton Elementary School?

5-27-05

Dear Fantastic Fifth Graders,

How do you feel on your last Friday of elementary school? I hope you are proud of all the work you've done. I also hope you have many great memories of Middleton. You are a great class, and I am proud of you.

Your teacher,
Mr. Henry

Draw a funny face:

At the end of the year teachers often use the message to sincerely celebrate a class. A heartfelt message such as this one will usually make a bigger impression on students if it's not written on the very last day of school.

A silly task lightens the tone of a serious message.

At their last morning meeting together, Eric reads the message aloud and asks each student to name the number of books he or she will try to read that summer.

June 1, 2005

Dear Fantastic Fifth Graders,

You worked hard this year, and I hope you have a great summer. Be sure to go outside as much as you can, and read at least ___ books! I'll miss you!

Sincerely,
Mr. Henry

A student spontaneously added this to the message.

We'll miss you, too!

Morning Meeting: Beginning Each Day as a Community of Learners

MORNING MEETING, a key element of the *Responsive Classroom®* approach to teaching, is a powerful tool for building community and integrating the teaching of social and academic skills. Morning Meeting, which takes place at the beginning of each school day, is a twenty- to thirty-minute gathering together of the children, their teacher, and sometimes other adults (such as special area teachers, other staff members, or parents). Sitting in a circle so that all can be seen and see everyone else, children and adults move through the four essential meeting components: greeting each other, sharing news, doing a group activity, and reading a message from the teacher that helps them look forward to the day ahead.

The four components of Morning Meeting intentionally provide opportunities for children to practice the skills of speaking, listening and responding, group problem solving, and noticing and anticipating, as well as academic skills they're working on. The components are done in the order shown here:

1. Greeting

Students make eye contact and greet each other by name. Greetings may consist of handshaking, singing, clapping, passing a Koosh ball, using a special wave, greeting in different languages, and many other variations on these ideas. The Greeting passes around the circle until everyone has been noticed and acknowledged, thus helping ensure that each child starts the day with positive recognition of her or his presence in the class.

2. Sharing

Students share information about events in their lives and then invite empathic comments or clarifying questions from listeners. To keep the meeting time manageable, only a few children share on any given day. Children may sign up to share, or the teacher may designate the day's sharers. Many methods of choosing sharers work well, as long as, over time, every child has opportunities to share. Through Sharing, children get to know one another better and develop bonds of trust with their classmates and teachers.

3. Group Activity

Everyone participates in a brief, lively activity that sometimes involves physical movement and often reinforces academic skills students have learned. This part of the Morning Meeting fosters group cohesion by continuing to emphasize inclusiveness and having fun together. Group Activity heightens the sense of community culture by building a class repertoire of shared songs, games, chants, and poems.

4. News and Announcements

During the final component of Morning Meeting, the class reviews the message their teacher has written for them that day. The message is designed with the group's particular academic goals and social needs in mind, and is intended to engage the children's interest and help them focus on the work of the day ahead. After reading the message together, the teacher leads a brief discussion or activity based on the message. The goal is to launch children into the day feeling confident and excited about learning together.

Presenting the components in this order is important. Greeting serves as a logical warm-up and tone-setter for Sharing, which requires that students feel a sense of comfort and trust in the group. The group must be feeling settled and calm for Sharing to work well. Group Activity follows Sharing because at this point in the meeting, the children are ready for the liveliness which whole-group involvement brings. News and Announcements helps to focus the group after the Activity and serves as a transition to the rest of the school day.

Within the meeting structure, teachers find plenty of opportunities to incorporate content relevant to the children's daily academic learning. Third graders working on multiplication, for example, might enjoy "beach ball math" for one meeting's Activity component. After writing numbers on each panel of the ball, children toss the ball to each other. Each catcher must multiply the numbers under each of her or his hands (asking for hints from classmates if needed), call out the answer, and toss the ball to another classmate. In a fourth grade classroom where students are studying fish, the teacher might write "Good Morning, Fish Researchers" as a morning mes-

sage salutation and describe something they'll be doing in science that day before inviting children to write a fact they know about a favorite fish.

The meeting structure also offers many opportunities to practice social skills. Children learn to greet others kindly, speak up clearly and confidently, listen respectfully, participate cooperatively with classmates who may be from very diverse backgrounds, and help each other. Meanwhile, children are fulfilling two basic human needs: to achieve a sense of belonging and significance, and to have fun.

For children, Morning Meetings offer a safe and enjoyable way to bolster critically important academic and social skills. For teachers, the meetings offer many opportunities to observe children's responses to social and academic challenges. From those observations come insights that can lead to more effective teaching.

Beginnings matter. The positive tone set by Morning Meeting creates the context not just for that single day in the classroom but for the children's developing understanding of school and of learning. Morning Meeting shows children, in words and actions, what it means to be part of a community of caring and respectful learners.

SUBJECT INDEX TO SAMPLE CHARTS

Language arts (See "Reading," "Skill practice," and "Writing")

Literacy (See "Reading," "Skill practice," and "Writing")

Mathematics 31, 41, 44, 45, 49, 50, 56, 63, 76, 77, 104, 113, 124, 127, 137, 140, 142 143, 199

Next year 87, 213, 214

Planning
    messages used for 39, 44, 70, 80, 83, 84, 85, 150, 177

Positive reinforcement
    messages giving 82, 84, 89, 173, 183, 188, 193, 196, 198, 215

Problem solving 67, 68, 179

Puzzles 52, 120, 184, 194, 200, 201, 219

Reading
    literature 48, 65, 66, 78, 111, 112, 117, 146, 149, 182, 222
    the message aloud at meeting 32, 109, 173
    sight words 50, 52
    (See also "Skill practice, reading")

Reflective thinking about
    accomplishments 131, 155, 183
    experience 47, 141, 156, 170, 217, 220
    learning 82, 131, 155, 196, 218

Science 36, 37, 40, 60, 64, 72, 73, 75, 79, 174, 178, 187, 194, 197

Skill practice
    handwriting 33, 39, 51, 59, 88
    letter and word finds 34, 41, 42, 55, 65, 141
    punctuation 43, 105, 116, 153, 168, 171, 215
    reading 29, 30, 35, 37, 42, 43, 74, 115, 123, 132, 135, 147, 194, 208
    spelling 122, 125, 134, 139, 186, 209, 217
    vocabulary 40, 45, 74, 77, 105, 120, 132, 135, 147, 181, 205

Social studies 119, 168, 183, 185, 191, 192, 200, 202, 207, 211

Special events 38, 48, 58, 88, 90, 106, 114, 154, 181, 195, 204
    (See also "Field trips" and "Classroom, visitors")

Spelling
    words used in message 116, 186
    standards for student responses 119

Substitute (or "guest") teachers 59, 66, 73, 114, 124, 128, 169, 173, 193, 201

Testing 82, 144, 203, 209

Vacation
    returning from 51, 63, 126, 138, 148, 188, 189, 190

Writing
    by students on the chart 30, 36, 41, 51, 71, 73, 103, 105, 110, 111, 123, 146
    preparing students for 81, 118, 130, 145, 151, 177, 185, 205, 206, 208, 209

About the *Responsive Classroom*® Approach

This book grew out of the work of Northeast Foundation for Children, Inc. (NEFC) and an approach to teaching known as the *Responsive Classroom* approach. Developed by classroom teachers, this approach consists of highly practical strategies for integrating social and academic learning throughout the school day.

SEVEN BELIEFS UNDERLIE THIS APPROACH:

1. The social curriculum is as important as the academic curriculum.

2. How children learn is as important as what they learn: Process and content go hand in hand.

3. The greatest cognitive growth occurs through social interaction.

4. There is a specific set of social skills that children need to learn and practice in order to be successful academically and socially: cooperation, assertion, responsibility, empathy, and self-control.

5. Knowing the children we teach—individually, culturally, and developmentally—is as important as knowing the content we teach.

6. Knowing the families of the children we teach and encouraging their participation is as important as knowing the children we teach.

7. How we, the adults at school, work together to accomplish our shared mission is as important as our individual competence: Lasting change begins with the adult community.

**More information and guidance on the
Responsive Classroom approach are available through:**

PUBLICATIONS AND RESOURCES

- Books and videos for elementary school educators

- Website with articles and other information:
  www.responsiveclassroom.org

- Free quarterly newsletter for elementary educators

PROFESSIONAL DEVELOPMENT OPPORTUNITIES

- One-day and week-long workshops for teachers

- Classroom consultations and other services at individual
  schools and school districts

- Multifaceted professional development for administrators
  and all staff at schools wishing to implement the *Responsive
  Classroom* approach school-wide

FOR DETAILS, CONTACT:

Northeast Foundation for Children, Inc.
85 Avenue A, Suite 204, P.O. Box 718
Turners Falls, MA 01376-0718

800-360-6332 Fax: 877-206-3952
www.responsiveclassroom.org

The Morning Meeting Book

By Roxann Kriete with contributions by Lynn Bechtel

For K–8 teachers (2002) 228 pages

Use Morning Meeting in your classroom to build community, increase students' investment in learning, and improve academic and social skills. This book features: ▪ Step-by-step guidelines for holding Morning Meeting ▪ A chapter on Morning Meeting in middle schools ▪ 45 greetings and 66 group activities ▪ Frequently asked questions and answers

The First Six Weeks of School

By Paula Denton and Roxann Kriete

For K–6 teachers (2000) 232 pages

Structure the first weeks of school to lay the groundwork for a productive year of learning. ▪ Guidelines for the first six weeks, including daily plans for the first three weeks for grades K–2, grades 3–4, and grades 5–6 ▪ Ideas for building community, teaching routines, introducing engaging curriculum, fostering autonomy ▪ Games, activities, greetings, songs, read-alouds, and resources especially useful during the early weeks of school

Classroom Spaces That Work

By Marlynn K. Clayton with Mary Beth Forton

For K–6 teachers (2001) 192 pages

Create a physical environment that is welcoming, well suited to the needs of students and teachers, and conducive to social and academic excellence. ▪ Practical ideas for arranging furniture ▪ Suggestions for selecting and organizing materials ▪ Ideas for creating displays ▪ Guidelines for setting up a meeting area ▪ Tips for making the space healthy

Rules in School
By Kathryn Brady, Mary Beth Forton, Deborah Porter, and Chip Wood
For K–8 teachers (2003) 272 pages

Establish a calm, safe learning environment and teach children self-discipline with this approach to classroom rules. ▪ Guidelines for creating rules with students based on their hopes and dreams for school ▪ Steps in modeling and role playing the rules ▪ How to reinforce the rules through language ▪ Using logical consequences when rules are broken ▪ Suggestions for teaching children to live by the rules outside the classroom

Learning Through Academic Choice
By Paula Denton, EdD
For K–6 teachers (2005) 224 pages

Enhance students' learning with this powerful tool for structuring lessons and activities. ▪ Information on building a strong foundation for Academic Choice ▪ Step-by-step look at Academic Choice in action ▪ Practical advice for creating an Academic Choice lesson plan ▪ Many ideas for Academic Choice activities

Parents and Teachers Working Together
By Carol Davis and Alice Yang
For K–6 teachers (2005) 232 pages

Build school-home cooperation and involve parents in ways that support their children's learning. ▪ Working with diverse family cultures ▪ Building positive relationships in the early weeks of school ▪ Keeping in touch all year long ▪ Involving parents in classroom life, including parents who can't physically come to school ▪ Problem-solving with parents